I Love Jesus & I Accept Evolution

I Love Jesus &
I Accept Evolution

DENIS O. LAMOUREUX

WIPF & STOCK · Eugene, Oregon

I LOVE JESUS & I ACCEPT EVOLUTION

Wipf and Stock Publishers
199 W. 8th Ave., Suite 3
Eugene, OR 97401

www.wipfandstock.com

ISBN 13: 978-1-55635-886-9

Manufactured in the U.S.A.

I DON'T THINK THAT there's any conflict at all between science today and the Scriptures. I think we have misinterpreted the Scriptures many times and we've tried to make the Scriptures say things that they weren't meant to say, and I think we have made a mistake by thinking the Bible is a scientific book. The Bible is not a book of science. The Bible is a book of Redemption, and of course, I accept the Creation story. I believe that God created man, and whether it came by an evolutionary process and at a certain point He took this person or being and made him a living soul or not, does not change the fact that God did create man. . . . whichever way God did it makes no difference as to what man is and man's relationship to God.

Billy Graham "Doubts and Certainties" (1964)

Contents

Contents

Figures

Figures

Acknowledgments

D URING THE WRITING OF my 500 page *Evolutionary Creation: A Christian Approach to Evolution* (2008), I recognized the need for a shorter and more accessible version of the book. *I Love Jesus & I Accept Evolution* is an attempt to outline the main points and arguments. Many who assisted me with the first book graciously agreed to contribute their time and expertise to this work.

Words cannot express how grateful I am to Anna-Lisa Ptolemy for her tireless and meticulous work on the early drafts of the manuscript. I also appreciated her insights on the anatomy of bird bones in chapter 5. Many thanks to Andrea Dmytrash, Braden Barr, and Kenneth Kully for their artwork. They were amazingly patient with me, and my incessant requests for changes to the diagrams. And I am thankful to my copy-editor Nancy Shoptaw. She purged the manuscript of excessive hyphens, capital letters, and Canadian-isms. The book is now in proper American, eh. Other wonderful friends and colleagues who provided support include: Edward Babinski, Chris Barrigar, Devadas Barrigar, Mike Beidler, Michael Caldwell, Joel Cannon, Bernie Dehler, Peter Enns, Trevor Froehlich, Jim Hoover, Murray Gingras, Nancy Halliday, Patrick Harrison, Margolee Horn, Marguerite and Ron Huggins, Douglas Jacoby, John Lang, Anthony Maiolo, Jack Maze, Terry Morrison, George Murphy, Amelia Reising, Jim Ruark, Anita and Paul Seely, Bethany Sollereder, Callee Soltys, Bonnie Topp, Martin Unsworth, Karima Yacoub, and Sharon Young.

DOL

February 12, 2009

Preface

THIS IS A TRUE story. A number of years ago I attended a conference on the relationship between science and religion at a leading university. One evening there was a public lecture that featured one of the most important anti-evolutionists in the country. During the question and answer period, a young man came to the microphone in front of about one thousand people. In a very respectful way, he asked a simple question, "What about dinosaurs, how do they fit into the Bible?"

I will never forget the answer that this university professor gave. In a mean-spirited tone, he scolded the young man, "This is an irrelevant question. It doesn't matter because it has nothing to do with what I'm saying tonight." And then there was dead silence. It was a very awkward and uncomfortable moment for everyone in the auditorium, including a number of individuals who were associated with this professor and his view of origins. In fact, I was sitting with a number of these anti-evolutionists. Without any response, the young man turned away from the microphone, walked up the aisle, and went out of the auditorium. No one got out of their seat to follow him. Not even one of the Christian anti-evolutionists with whom I was seated.

But I immediately sensed the Lord calling me to comfort this young man. Yes, me, of all people, an evolutionist! I went out to the foyer and found him. He was shaking like a leaf. I introduced myself as a university professor and complemented him on what I thought was an excellent question. And then he said to me with trembling voice, "All I wanted to know from Dr. _____ was where do dinosaurs fit into the Bible, because I would like to tell my high school friends." Wow! Here was a 16- or 17-year-old boy who had the courage to stand up before a large audience at a major university and ask a question that he believed would help his *high school* classmates understand the relationship between Scripture and science. He wanted to explain and defend his Christian faith to his friends.

I realized I had a problem. I had just affirmed this student's question, but how would I explain in only a few minutes where dinosaurs fit into the Bible? My university career has focused on the modern origins debate and questions like this one. But there are no quick and easy answers. I felt handcuffed. Standing before me was a teenager who, along with his classmates, had grown up watching the *Jurassic Park* movies. They all know that dinosaurs once existed. And here was a young man with a solid faith and a question that undoubtedly many Christians his age have asked. I wanted to tell him that I love Jesus and that I accept evolution. But this was not the right thing to say at that volatile moment. It would only have added to the confusion. All I could do was affirm his wonderful faith, remarkable courage, and intellectual integrity. I told him that loving God with our mind, as Jesus has commanded us, requires that we ask tough questions like the one he had just asked the speaker. I knew he wanted more, but I couldn't deliver it.

This honest question and shameful answer still echo in my soul years later. As a matter of fact, they have inspired me to write this book. In many ways, it is my attempt at offering a response to this high school student and his classmates. The answer that I give will surprise a lot of Christians. First, I will suggest that the purpose of the Bible is not to reveal scientific facts about how God created the world. To use the words of Billy Graham in the epigraph at the front of this book, "The Bible is not a book of science."[1] In the same way that the Lord meets each of us wherever we happen to be, the Holy Spirit came down to the level of the ancient biblical writers and used their understanding of nature to reveal that He was the Creator of the entire world. The intention of the biblical creation accounts is to disclose spiritual truths for nourishing our personal relationship with Jesus.

Second, I will propose that God created the universe and life through evolution. This view of origins is known as "evolutionary creation." It claims that evolution is a creative process similar to that which the Lord uses to form every one of us in our mother's womb. No Christian today believes that God comes out of heaven to attach an ear, nose, or arm to a developing baby. Instead, we understand that He employs natural processes to create human beings. In fact, God is the creator of all the laws of nature, including these developmental (embryological) mechanisms. I believe that this is also the case with evolution. The Creator planned and maintained evolutionary laws and processes in order to create the entire world and us. In other words, our origin is not a fluke or mistake.

My view of origins is built on the traditional Christian belief that the Lord reveals Himself through Two Divine Books. First, the Book of God's Words is the Bible. It discloses that we are the only creatures who were made in the Image of God, and that our Creator loves us more that we can ever imagine. I personally understand the power of Scripture. By reading the gospel of John, I was born again thirty years ago. Experiencing the fact that Jesus died for our sins and then rose physically from the grave changed my life completely and forever. Today, I drink from the Bible every morning for my spiritual nourishment in order to strengthen my personal relationship with the Lord. Second, the Book of God's Works is the natural world. Modern science examines its structure, operation, and origin. Microscopes and telescopes assist in revealing that the creation is incredibly amazing! Beauty, complexity, and functionality in nature point to the mind of God. Stated in another way, the universe and life reflect intelligent design.

The Two Divine Books complement each other in revealing the glory and character of the Creator. I will propose an intimate and fruitful relationship between Biblical faith and evolutionary science. Scripture discloses the spiritual character of the world, while science reveals the divine method of creation. To be sure, such a provocative claim is rarely heard in our churches. This might be offensive to some. But no insult is intended, and I will ask my brothers and sisters in Christ for their patience as they read this book.

In order to understand my view of origins, I strongly advise that the chapters be read in sequence. The conclusions in later chapters are dependent on the terms and ideas presented in earlier ones. There is a short glossary at the back of the book to assist readers with the terminology. I suggest that they introduce themselves to these concepts before starting chapter 1.

No doubt about it, *I Love Jesus & I Accept Evolution* is a challenging book for most Christians. Readers must be warned that I will make a number of pointed and even disturbing statements, especially with regard to the meaning of several biblical passages. You will be uncomfortable at times. However, there is a generation of young Christian men and women who want to know where dinosaurs fit into the Bible. This is not an irrelevant question. Rather, it's a very important one. And I believe that asking tough and honest questions is part of the commandment to love God with our mind (Matt 22:37). Hopefully, this book will make a modest contribution in offering some answers on origins and Christian faith.

1

Terms and Definitions

I AM OFTEN ASKED, "Are you an evolutionist or a creationist?" After a bit of a pause, I answer, "Well, I happen to be both." A look of disbelief then quickly appears on the face of the person asking the question. Similarly, many have asked, "Do you believe in evolution or intelligent design?" Again, my response is puzzling to most individuals: "I accept evolution and I definitely see the beauty, complexity, and functionality in nature as indicative of the work of an Intelligent Designer." Once more, people are troubled, and they swiftly respond, "But that doesn't make sense." Regrettably, on a few occasions some have even said that they doubt I'm a Christian. Why? Because many believe that Christians can't be evolutionists.

No doubt about it, given the common definitions of the terms evolution, creation, and intelligent design, my views on origins are contradictory. But this is where I think a serious problem exists with the origins debate today. Most people come to this discussion with black-and-white terminology. The word "evolution" is chained to a godless worldview that rejects intelligent design in nature; the term "creation" is fused to origins in six literal days as found in the Bible. This blending or collapsing of terms into one idea is known as "conflation," and it severely restricts the meaning of words. Consequently, many assume that there are only two possibilities with regard to origins—one is either an evolutionist or a creationist. This setting up of an issue into only two simple positions is called a "dichotomy." It forces people to choose between one of two choices, and it blinds them from seeing the wide range of possibilities on how God could have created the world.

I certainly appreciate why most Christians and non-Christians state that my views make no sense. For dozens of years, I myself was trapped

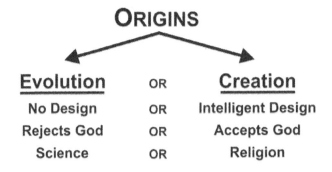

Fig 1-1. The Origins Dichotomy

in the origins dichotomy. I came from a Christian home and entered college believing that God created the world in six 24-hour days. But once I saw the evidence for evolution in biology classes, the either/or approach to origins soon led me to reject my faith. Like everyone around me, I conflated evolution with atheism. Our black-and-white thinking about origins had us believe that it was impossible to accept both evolution and Christianity. As a result, most of us thought that science and religion were at war. And in my senior year of college, I became an atheist.

In coming back to Jesus and the church a few years after college, I was still entrenched in this wretched dichotomy. I experienced a powerful born-again conversion by reading the gospel of John. (Isn't it amazing how often people come to Christ by reading this gospel?) Yet this time, my either/or understanding of origins led me to reject evolution. Like most in my church, I believed that evolution was Satan's lie for leading men and women away from the Bible and the Lord. I continued to conflate the term creation with a strict literal reading of the first chapters of Scripture. And I still assumed that there was an endless conflict between science and religion. In fact, I left my career as a dentist and entered graduate school with the intention of declaring war on everyone who accepted evolution! Fig 1-1 presents the origins dichotomy.

Clearly, my story of flipping and flopping between evolution and creation reveals a serious problem with the popular understanding of terminology that controls the origins debate today. This chapter introduces terms and definitions that free readers from commonly conflated words, and it assists them in moving beyond the simplistic origins dichotomy. In this way, each of us is able to make informed decisions as we develop our view on the origin of the universe and life.

EVOLUTION

Most people associate the term evolution with a biological theory of molecules-to-people that is driven only by blind chance. This word is conflated with an atheistic worldview—the belief that God does not exist and that our existence has no ultimate meaning or purpose. Understandably, this popular use of evolution produces strong negative reactions within the church. But for some Christians, evolution is simply the method through which the Lord created life, including humans who bear His Image. These believers argue that God employed a set of natural mechanisms for the creation of every living organism that has ever existed on earth in the same way that He uses physical processes to create each one of us in our mother's womb.

Therefore, there are two radically different meanings of the word evolution, and in order to avoid confusion, qualification is necessary. On the one hand, "teleological evolution" is a planned and purposeful natural process that heads toward a final outcome—the intended creation of life. The Greek word *telos* means end, goal, or final destiny. On the other hand, "dysteleological evolution" is an unplanned and purposeless series of physical mechanisms driven by blind chance only. According to this approach, evolutionary processes unintentionally generated living organisms, including humans. In other words, we are just a fluke of nature. The term *dysteleologie* was first coined in German and refers to a worldview without any ultimate plan or purpose. This bleak belief asserts that existence is marked by nothing but pointless indifference with no ultimate right or wrong.

Teleological evolution is connected to the notion of intelligent design in nature. History reveals that the world's beauty, complexity, and functionality have powerfully impacted men and women throughout time. For most of us, this experience has led to the conclusion that the universe and life reflect the work of a rational mind, thus arguing for the existence of a Creator. Teleological evolutionists contend that the natural processes of evolution also reveal intelligent design. In contrast, dysteleological evolutionists believe that design in nature is nothing but a delusion concocted by the human mind. Of course, these skeptics acknowledge that there is striking elegance, intricacy, and efficiency in the world, but they argue that this experience is only an "appearance" of design, which most people misunderstand and impose upon nature. Fig 1-2 presents these two definitions of the term evolution.

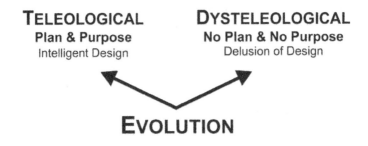

TELEOLOGICAL
Plan & Purpose
Intelligent Design

DYSTELEOLOGICAL
No Plan & No Purpose
Delusion of Design

EVOLUTION

Fig 1-2. Re-Categorization of the Term Evolution

Regrettably, the origins dichotomy has forced many Christians to cast suspicion on science and the scientific community, because to them the word evolution is essentially atheistic or dysteleological. But this is a popular myth that needs to be debunked. A 1997 study of American scientists reveals that 40% believe in life after death and a God who answers prayer in a way that is "more than the subjective, psychological effect of prayer."[1] In other words, a significant number of scientists believe in a personal God that intervenes in their life in a miraculous way. Thus, at least 4 out of 10 scientists have a teleological worldview. In addition, 15% of those surveyed did not have an opinion regarding personal divine action. Therefore, 55% of US scientists are definitely not atheistic or dysteleological.

It is important to underline that when scientists use the term evolution in their day-to-day research, they rarely mention whether they believe this natural process is planned and designed by a Creator, or purposeless and driven only by blind chance. Science deals only with the laws and processes of the physical world. Scientific methods and instruments cannot detect teleology or dysteleology. Consequently, science is dead silent on the ultimate religious and philosophical character of evolution. Of course, like everyone else, scientists ponder the meaning of life and reflect upon nature in their quest to understand existence. But such spiritual and intellectual contemplation extends beyond science and into the realms of religion and philosophy. We will examine this issue in more detail later in the intelligent design section of this chapter.

In light of the previous points, the definition of the term evolution used in science today is as follows: evolution is a scientific theory that asserts that the universe and life, including humans, arose through natural processes. There are three basic evolutionary sciences. "Cosmological evolution" examines the development of the inanimate world with its galaxies, stars, and planets. Physicists state that an explosive event 10–15 billion years ago, termed the "Big Bang," led to the origin of space, time, and matter. "Geological evolution" investigates the formation of the earth. Geologists reconstruct the 4.5 billion-year history of our planet in light of the physical processes that are ongoing today, such as erosion, volcanic activity, continental drift, etc. "Biological evolution" describes and explains the origin of life as seen in the fossil record, beginning about 4 billion years ago. Biologists explore the natural mechanisms that organized inanimate molecules into the first living forms and that later led to the evolution of all plants and animals, including human beings.

A comment is needed regarding the term "Darwinism." For most individuals, it refers to dysteleological evolution. This popular definition conflates Charles Darwin's understanding of evolution with an atheistic worldview. But this is another popular myth that needs to be burst. In his famed *On the Origin of Species* (1859), Darwin presents a teleological interpretation of evolution and makes seven affirmative references to the Creator. For example, he argues:

> Authors of the highest eminence [i.e., leading scientists in Darwin's day] seem to be fully satisfied that each species has been independently created. To my mind it accords better with what we know of the laws impressed on matter by the Creator, that the production and extinction of the past and present inhabitants of the world should have been due to secondary causes like those determining the birth and death of the individual.[2]

Notably, Darwin saw a parallel between God's creative activity in embryology and evolution. He contended that the Creator had made laws of nature that led to both the creation of an individual in the womb and the origin of all species on earth. Darwin's position in 1859 is proof that the origins dichotomy is a *false dichotomy*. He believed in both God and evolution. In fact, only a few years before his death in 1882, he openly admitted, "I have never been an atheist in the sense of denying the existence of God."[3] Therefore, in order to limit confusion and misunderstanding, I suggest that the term Darwinism not be used in the origins debate.

To summarize, caution is necessary when using or reading the word evolution because it carries a number of meanings. The popular use of this term is conflated with an atheistic and dysteleological worldview. However, the professional definition of evolution employed by scientists refers only to the scientific theory that describes and explains the origin of the world through natural mechanisms, with no mention of the religious or philosophical character of these physical processes. In the origins debate, the word evolution often needs to be qualified with the adjectives teleological or dysteleological.

CREATION

The popular understanding of the term creation also contributes to the entrenchment of the origins dichotomy. Most people consider a creationist to be an individual who believes that God created the universe and life in six 24-hour days as described by a strict literal reading of Gen 1. In other words, the concept of creation is conflated with *one* interpretation of this biblical chapter. Regrettably, this leads to the common perception both inside and outside the church that six-day creation is the "official" Christian view of origins. However, in recent years there has been a quiet shift in the thinking of a number of believers. Many today accept cosmological and geological evolution, which date the universe to be billions of years old. As a result, the terms "young earth creation" and "old earth creation" now appear in our churches.

God's creative method is not a central topic among theologians, even though many Christians believe that it is fundamental to the faith. Of course, these scholars are interested in how the world originated, but they know that science is not their expertise. According to theologians, the term creation refers only to that which God has made. Similarly, a creationist is simply someone who believes in a Creator.

Today, Christian theologians uphold the theological doctrine of creation and assert that it is a religious belief and not a scientific theory. This doctrine is based on Scripture and features seven basic principles:

- The creation is radically distinct and different from the Creator (Gen 1:1; John 1:1–3; Heb 1:10–12; Rev 1:8). The entire universe is not God; nor is any part of the world divine. The Creator transcends the creation. Yet He is also imminent to His works (omnipresent) and knows their every detail (omniscient). And God enters into the world to interact with His creatures at any time and in any way He so chooses (omnipotent).

- The creation is utterly dependent on the Creator (Job 34:14–15; Pss 65:9–13, 104:1–35; Acts 17:24–28; Col 1:16–17; Heb 1:2–3; Rev 4:11). God *ordained* the universe and life into being, and He continues to *sustain* their existence during every single instant. The ultimate meaning of the cosmos is rooted in the Creator. He has ordered a plan and purpose for the world. More precisely, the teleological character of the creation is completely dependent on God.

- The creation was made out of nothing (Rom 4:17; 1 Cor 8:6; Col 1:15–17; Heb 2:10, 11:3). The Creator did not fashion the universe from eternal pre-existent material. Nor was there any timeless being or force to challenge His lordship. God existed before all things and powers, both visible and invisible.

- The creation is temporal (Gen 1:1; John 1:1–3; Matt 24:35; 2 Pet 3:7, 12–13). God not only created physical matter and empty space, but also time. In other words, the universe is not eternal. It is bound in time and has both a beginning and an end that are determined by the Creator.

- The creation declares God's glory (Job 38–41; Ps 19:1–4; Rom 1:19–20). The Creator has written a transcendent message into the physical world. Known as "natural revelation," this divine disclosure is similar to the universal language of music in that it is non-verbal (Latin *verbum*: word). That is, it does not use actual words. But this revelation in nature clearly communicates that the universe and life are the work of God, and it even reveals some of His attributes, such as His divine nature and eternal power. In particular, the elegance, intricacy, and efficiency of the creation reflect intelligent design, pointing to the mind of our Maker.

- The creation is very good (Gen 1:31; 1 Tim 4:4; Rom 8:28). The world offers the perfect stage for the Creator's will to unfold. It includes a myriad of amazing features—joys and hardships, frustrations and freedoms, thrills and dangers, beauty and ugliness, love and hate, sin and grace—all intended by God to work for good and to give Him glory. In particular, this is an ideal cosmos for experiencing love and developing relationships among ourselves, and between us and our Maker.

- The creation features a living being that bears the Image of God (Gen 1:26–27, 9:6). Men and women are the crown of creation. We are unique in that no other creature enjoys such a privileged and honored status as bearing the precious Image of the Creator.

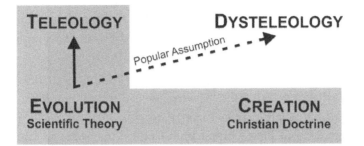

Fig 1-3. Evolutionary Creation: A Christian Approach to Evolution. The popular assumption both inside and outside the church is that evolution is dysteleological and driven only by blind chance. In contrast, evolutionary creation (shaded area) asserts that evolution is teleological. The God of Christianity created the universe and life through an ordained, sustained, and intelligent design-reflecting natural process.

To sum up, care is needed with the word creation since it carries many meanings today. The popular use of this term usually refers to six-day creation, giving the impression that this is the only acceptable Christian position on origins. However, such an approach conflates a strict literal interpretation of Gen 1 with the word creation. The definition of this term employed by professional theologians refers only to the beings and things that the Creator has created, and not to His creative method. In other words, the Christian doctrine of creation does not focus on *how* God created, but *that* God created.

Considering the definitions of evolution and creation presented above, biblical faith and evolutionary science can be viewed in a new light. It is reasonable to accept both the Christian doctrine of creation and the scientific theory of evolution. From this perspective, the God of the Bible created the world through teleological evolution, which is a design-reflecting natural process that He ordained and sustained. Fig 1-3 outlines this fresh approach to origins, termed "evolutionary creation."

INTELLIGENT DESIGN

The belief that nature reflects intelligent design appears throughout history.* The beauty, complexity, and functionality of the world have powerfully

---

* It is important to distinguish the biblical and traditional understanding of intelligent design from the view of design being promoted today by the Intelligent Design Movement (or Intelligent Design Theory). The latter is a narrow view of design and claims that design is connected to miraculous interventions in the origin of life. For example, parts of the cell like the flagellum are said to be "irreducibly complex," and as a result, they could not

impacted most people and led them to conclude that these features point to the mind of a Creator. This idea is not uniquely Christian. It transcends times and cultures, religions and philosophies, even intellectual abilities and educational backgrounds. Design in nature has been proclaimed in the past by inspired biblical authors and ancient philosophers, and in the present by world-class scientists and anyone who enjoys looking up at the starry heavens. The argument from design is one of the most powerful defenses for the existence of God.

Biblical Support for Intelligent Design

The Bible acknowledges that intelligent design is real and that humans have the ability to understand this natural revelation in the Book of God's Works. The best biblical evidence supporting the notion of design is found in Ps 19:1–4 and Rom 1:18–20. Together, these passages assert that an intelligible, non-verbal, and divine revelation exists in the creation; that this disclosure points to God, revealing some of His attributes; and that humanity is accountable before the Creator with regard to the implications of this revelation inscribed in nature.

In Ps 19:1–4, the psalmist records:

> ¹The heavens declare the glory of God;
>   the skies proclaim the work of His hands.
> ²Day after day they pour forth speech;
>   night after night they display knowledge.
> ³There is no speech or language
>   where their voice is not heard.
> ⁴Their voice goes out into all the earth,
>   their words to the ends of the world.

This passage identifies five features in the Book of Nature: (1) The creation is *active*. The repeated use of verbs in the active voice (i.e., the subject performs an action) underlines that the physical world thrusts a revelation upon us. The heavens "declare," the skies "proclaim," both "pour forth" and "display," and their voice "goes out." (2) This activity flowing from nature is *intelligible*. The disclosure is characterized by terms associated with intelligent communication: "speech," "language," "knowledge," "voice," and "words." (3) The creation's message is *incessant*. It is heard

---

have evolved through natural processes. Since this is the case, ID Theory should be termed *Interventionistic* Design Theory. In contrast, I will focus on the scriptural and Christian view of intelligent design, which simply states that the creation impacts everyone, declaring God's glory and revealing His eternal power and divine nature.

"day after day" and "night after night" throughout time. (4) This cosmic revelation is *universal*. Like music, "there is no speech or language where their voice is not heard," and it travels "into all the earth" and "to the ends of the world." Because it does not use actual words, everyone understands this non-verbal disclosure in the creation. (5) The message woven into the fabric of the cosmos is *divine* or *transcendent*. It "declares the glory of God" and "proclaims the work of His hands." Nature clearly points to the existence of a Creator.

Romans 1:18–20 reiterates the characteristics of natural revelation presented in Ps 19. The apostle Paul writes:

> [18]The wrath of God is being revealed from heaven against all the godlessness and wickedness of men who suppress the truth by their wickedness, [19]since what may be known about God is plain to them, because God has made it plain to them. [20]For since the creation of the world God's invisible qualities—His eternal power and divine nature—have been clearly seen, being understood from what has been made, so that men are without excuse.

Five features in the Book of God's Works include: (1) The creation is *active*. The revelatory impact of "what has been made" is so powerful that men and women are completely accountable before God. (2) This activity arising from nature is *intelligible*. It is described using verbs associated with intelligent communication: "known," "seen," and "understood." (3) The creation's message is *incessant*. It has flowed out ever "since the creation of the world." (4) This cosmic revelation is *universal*. Non-verbal knowledge in nature has been "made plain" in order to be "clearly seen" by everyone "so that men are without excuse." (5) The message engraved deeply into the cosmos is *divine* or *transcendent*. In particular, the creation reveals some characteristics of God, such as "His eternal power and divine nature."

However, in Rom 1 Paul goes further than the psalmist and introduces a sixth feature of natural revelation—the creation is *judgmental*. The clear and intelligible divine message in nature makes humanity accountable and "without excuse" regarding its profound consequence. Accordingly, there is no justification for "godlessness and wickedness" since the creation is a constant witness declaring the existence of a powerful and divine Creator. Yet, this inexcusability implies that people are free to dismiss and ignore the message in nature. Like the gospel of Jesus in the Book of God's Words, the natural revelation in the Book of God's Works does not force men and women into becoming believers. They can reject it and its Author, if they so choose.

Relating Science and Religion: An Approach to Intelligent Design

In light of this biblical evidence that affirms the reality of intelligent design, it is clear that design is a foundational issue in developing a healthy relationship between science and religion. Moving beyond the so-called "warfare" begins by respecting the basic differences between scientific methods and religious faith. In this way, science and religion can complement each other and contribute to understanding our existence.

Science deals with the physical world. It investigates the structure, operation, and origin of the universe and life. Through observations and experiments, scientists advance theories and establish laws to describe *what* nature is made of and *how* it works. Science focuses on natural causes. In contrast, religion (and philosophy) examines the ultimate meaning of the world. It deals with the deepest questions humans have ever asked: *Why* does the world exist? *Who* or *what* is behind the universe, if anyone or anything? Do beauty, complexity, and functionality in nature reflect intelligent design, or are these irrelevant features that lead to the delusion of design? Religion and philosophy concentrate on final and ultimate causes. To employ terms derived from Greek, science investigates *phusis*, which translated literally means "nature," and from which are derived the English words "physics" and "physical." Religion and philosophy explore *metaphusis* or metaphysics. The Greek preposition *meta* means "behind," "beyond," and "after." Thus, metaphysics deals with the ultimate reality behind or beyond the physical world after it has been examined and studied.

Fig 1-4 presents the Metaphysics-Physics Principle and depicts the intimate relationship between science and religion/philosophy. In the lower half of the diagram, science offers vast and wonderful knowledge about nature. But it is dead silent with regard to the ultimate meaning of the physical world. There is no scientific instrument that can detect whether or not the cosmos is teleological or dysteleological, or whether or not the elegant complexity in nature is intelligently designed. Such topics are metaphysical and dealt with only in religion and philosophy, as depicted in the upper half of the diagram. However, theologians and philosophers depend on science in coming to their deepest beliefs. They

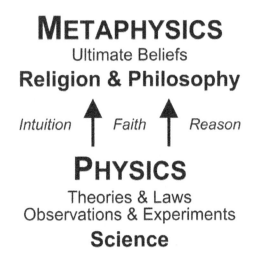

METAPHYSICS
Ultimate Beliefs
Religion & Philosophy

Intuition ⬆ *Faith* ⬆ *Reason*

PHYSICS
Theories & Laws
Observations & Experiments
Science

Fig 1-4. The Metaphysics-Physics Principle

need facts about the natural world before they can decide on its ultimate meaning. Stated concisely, metaphysics requires physics.

Fig 1-4 also presents the basic operating dynamic between science and religion. In order to arrive at ultimate beliefs, everyone must "jump" upward from the scientific data. This is not merely a strict logical process like mathematics. In fact, there is no mathematical formula to move from physics to metaphysics. Of course, the jump does involve reason, a logically thought out process that is objective in character. But it also includes intuition, an immediate impression that is more subjective. Together, reason and intuition contribute to faith, and this intellectual-spiritual process leads to an ultimate belief regarding the discoveries of science. Indeed, this jump may legitimately be called a "leap of faith" because that is exactly what it is. To use the biblical definition of faith, "Faith is being sure of what we hope for and certain of what we do not see" (Heb 11:1). No one today can prove the metaphysical status of the physical world with absolute and total certainty. It is a belief. And everyone makes this metaphysical jump, whether they are aware of it or not, and whether they are religious or not. In other words, we are all believers in some sort of ultimate truth, and we all embrace some sort of faith.

The cell in biology provides an example to explore the Metaphysics-Physics Principle and to understand intelligent design.* Science has dis-

---

* There are an incalculable number of other illustrations in nature that I could use to make my point. For example, physics reveals that the Big Bang was delicately balanced to

covered that the diameter of an average cell is roughly 1/1000th of an inch. If placed on the tip of a pin, the naked eye cannot see it. In this cell, there is about 1 yard of DNA that is tightly coiled into a number of chromosomes. The information encoded in this genetic material is approximately equivalent to that of a 30-volume encyclopedia. This is standard scientific data and no scientist, whether religious or not, questions these physical facts of biology. In fact, all professional biologists acknowledge the incredible beauty, complexity, and functionality of the cell. Such information characterizes knowledge in science as depicted in the lower half of the diagram in Fig 1-4.

But an especially revealing situation emerges when religious and non-religious scientists ponder the ultimate meaning of this biological data. They come to completely opposite metaphysical beliefs. In jumping from the physical evidence in the lower half of the diagram to their metaphysical position in the upper half, religious believers argue that the cell's elegance, intricacy, and efficiency reflect intelligent design. That is, their reason and intuition lead them to the belief that the cell ultimately features teleology and points to an Intelligent Designer. In contrast, non-religious scientists assessing the identical biological facts acknowledge these physical features in cells, but they leap to the belief that this data offers only delusions of design and teleology. In other words, these individuals have faith that this scientific data is ultimately dysteleological.

Of course, the question immediately arises: How do we account for this radical difference between religious and non-religious scientists in their appraisal of the metaphysical character of the cell? Clearly, a powerful and determinative factor beyond simple logic is operating because both groups agree on the use of logic. After all, it led them to the very same physical facts about the cell. I have come to the conclusion that *the central factor influencing the "jump" from the scientific data to the assessment of this data's ultimate meaning is spiritual—it deals directly with the impact of sin on the human mind.*

---

one part in 10^{60} (i.e., 1 part in 1,000,000,000,000,000,000,000,000,000,000,000,000,00 0,000,000,000,000,000,000). If the explosive force was greater by this unfathomably small fraction, galaxies would not have formed; if the gravitational force was slightly stronger by this same amount, the universe would have re-collapsed on itself. This fine tuning of the laws of nature is known as the "anthropic principle" (Greek *anthrōpos*: man, human being). It claims that from the very first moments, the physical world seems to be set up in order to produce an environment that is suitable for humans.

In Rom 1:21–23, Paul offers insight into the intellectual-spiritual dynamic of the relationship between science and religion. He notes that the rejection of natural revelation is intimately connected to an individual's spiritual condition and relationship with God. After stating that men and women are "without excuse" regarding the clear disclosure of the Creator in nature (v. 20), the apostle writes:

> [21]For although they knew God, they neither glorified Him as God nor gave thanks to Him, but their thinking became futile and their foolish hearts were darkened. [22]Although they claimed to be wise, they became fools and [23]exchanged the glory of the immortal God for images made to look like mortal man and birds and animals and reptiles.

Failure to glorify God or to give Him thanks results in futile thinking and idolatry. In other words, violation of the First Commandment ("You shall have no other gods before Me" Exod 20:3; Deut 5:7) leads to breaking the Second Commandment ("You shall not make yourself an idol in the form of anything in the heaven above or on the earth beneath or in the waters below," Exod 20:5; Deut 5:8). Romans 1 clearly states that sin produces intellectual dysfunction. Therefore, it is not surprising that the reflection of intelligent design as revealed by science today would be perverted, disregarded, or rationalized away by those not wanting to acknowledge the Creator's existence and their accountability before Him.

To be sure, intelligent design in nature has profoundly personal and life-changing implications. Not only does the divine message in the Book of Nature declare God's creatorship, but it also proclaims His lordship over the entire world, including each and every one of us. As a biologist, I am blown away by the elegance, intricacy, and efficiency that I see in living organisms. But as a theologian, I recognize that the impacting force of nature is not a scientific *proof* for the existence of God. Rather, this powerful experience is an excellent *argument* for an Intelligent Designer. In the end, believing or disbelieving that nature points to a Creator is an act of faith. The atheists might be right in claiming that design is a delusion, but I doubt that they are correct. I think that it takes more faith, in fact blind faith, to believe that random chance made our amazing and wonderful world, rather than to believe in God.

SCIENTIFIC CONCORDISM

Christians in every generation have drunk deeply from the Bible for their spiritual nourishment. They recognize that "all Scripture is God-breathed" (2 Tim 3:16) and that it contains "the very words of God" (Rom 3:2). An assumption held by many believers is that the Creator revealed scientific facts in Scripture thousands of years before their discovery by modern science. This view of biblical inspiration asserts that the Holy Spirit dictated information about the natural world to secretary-like writers. As a result, numerous Christians believe that there is an alignment or correspondence between the Bible and science. This purported feature in the Word of God is commonly known as "concordism," but I prefer to qualify it as "scientific concordism."

The belief that there is an accord between Scripture and science is a very reasonable expectation. After all, God is both the Author of His Words and the Creator of His Works. It is perfectly logical to assume that the Two Divine Books line up with each other. Christians embracing scientific concordism claim that the science in the Bible is powerful evidence that proves the supernatural character of God's Word. They argue that only an all-knowing Creator who transcends time could have given such a revelation ahead of time. Moreover, these believers assert that there are no scientific errors in the Bible. In other words, scientific concordists contend that the statements about the physical world in Scripture are inerrant, and as such are foundational to the belief in biblical inerrancy.

It is inevitable that a generation of Christians who have been raised in a scientific age would want to correlate their faith with modern science, especially in regards to the origin of the universe and life. Indeed, nearly 90% of born-again Christians in the United States believe that the biblical creation accounts reveal scientific facts on how God made the world.[4] However, there are difficulties with the scientific concordist method of interpretation if the Holy Spirit, in offering a revelation about the creation, used a writing style that is not a straightforward as-it-happened account of origins. It is also reasonable to suggest that God, as a loving Father, came down to the level of the ancient Hebrews and spoke to them using their own science in order to communicate as effectively as possible. That is, in the same way that the Lord meets us wherever we happen to be and speaks to us in terms that we can understand, He also spoke to ancient Israel, employing ideas about the natural world that she comprehended.

From this perspective, the Holy Spirit may well have *accommodated* to the mindset of the inspired biblical authors and their readers.

In order to explore whether Scripture features scientific concordism or an accommodation to the ancient Hebrews, it is critical to identify two fundamental types of statements in the Bible. First and foremost, the Word of God features theological statements. The central purpose of biblical revelation is to reveal the Creator, including His will, acts, and character. Scripture also discloses the spiritual (or metaphysical) character of the physical world. The universe and life are very good creations of God (Gen 1:1, 31) and they reflect His glory, workmanship, and divine nature (Ps 19:1; Rom 1:20). Most significantly, the Bible reveals the two defining spiritual characteristics of humanity—we bear the Image of God and we are sinful (Gen 1:26–27; Gen 3; Rom 3:23). Second, Scripture also makes many statements about the structure, operation, and origin of the world. These can certainly be termed "scientific" statements because they are assertions about nature. For example, Isa 40:22 refers to "the circle of the earth," Eccl 1:5 states that "the sun rises and the sun sets, and hurries back to where it rises," and Gen 2:7 clearly claims that God made the first man "from the dust of the ground."

Since the Bible includes both theological and scientific statements, it could be argued that there are two basic types of biblical concordism. "Theological concordism" claims that there is an indispensable correspondence between the theological truths in Scripture and spiritual reality. "Scientific concordism" states that there is an alignment between the assertions about nature in the Bible and the physical world. Notably, some topics such as human origins feature overlapping statements. For example, the book of Genesis asserts the spiritual truth that men and women were created in God's Image (1:26–27); it also makes the scientific claim that Adam was the first man of the human race, leading many Christians to believe that we did not evolve from lower forms of life (2:7). Fig 1-5 depicts two basic categories of biblical concordism.

Interesting questions arise with regard to the different types of statements in Scripture. First, do the theological and scientific statements in the Bible actually correspond to spiritual reality and the physical world, respectively? Our rational and psychological needs press upon us to expect some sort of agreement if we believe the Bible to be true and relevant to our lives. However, should modern scientific discoveries not align with statements about nature in Scripture, are Christians forced to choose between science and the Bible? Stated another way, does such a situation

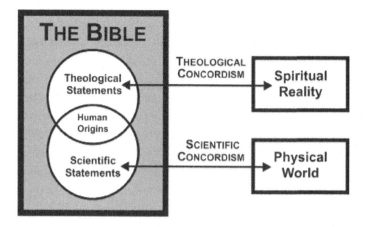

Fig 1-5. Categories of Biblical Concordism. The structure of this diagram reflects the Metaphysics-Physics Principle (Fig 1-4). Theological statements are metaphysical, and scientific statements deal only with physical reality.

force individuals into a dichotomy: either embracing blind faith or rejecting Christianity? Moreover, does biblical inerrancy extend to both theological and scientific concordism? Or can inerrancy be limited to only the spiritual statements in the Word of God, and not include assertions about the structure, operation, and origin of the physical world?

Second, how do the theological and scientific statements in the Bible relate to one another? It is clear from Fig 1-5 why the topic of human origins is such a critical and explosive issue for Christians. The origin of humanity deals with both types of biblical statements. But is this overlap essential and indispensable? Or is it only incidental and reflective of the ancient period when these statements were written down? Asked more precisely, are the theological and scientific claims regarding human origins necessarily connected? Or, are these two types of statements, in principle, independent of each other, having been put together by inspired ancient writers under the accommodating guidance of the Holy Spirit? In addition, do the theological assertions in Scripture about the origin of men and women require proof from modern science for them to be true? Is it possible to develop a biblically based theology about humanity without Scripture's scientific statements on human origins?

I will deal directly with these important and challenging questions in this book. I contend that two powerful factors fuel the so-called "evolution vs. creation" debate. First, many Christians cling firmly to scientific concordism in the biblical accounts of origins, specifically Gen 1–3. Second, they conflate this type of concordism with the notion of biblical inerrancy. Regrettably, this conflation has produced a blind spot in the mind of Christians that prohibits them from envisioning how God could have created the world through evolution. It must be noted that many non-Christians also assume that biblical faith depends on scientific concordism in the opening chapters of Genesis, and they too stoke the origins controversy and deepen the dichotomy between science and religion.

In proposing a solution, I will use the Word of God itself to show that scientific concordism fails. The science in the Bible is an ancient science. It is the science-of-the-day a few thousand years ago in the ancient Near East. Therefore, any attempt to align modern science with biblical statements about the origin of the world is doomed to fail. In addition, I tenaciously defend that theological concordism is the essential feature of the biblical creation accounts. The primary purpose of Gen 1–3 is to start the process of revealing God and His unconditional love for all of us, and therefore, biblical inerrancy resides in the theological statements disclosed by the Holy Spirit. I will also suggest that the ancient science in Scripture is an incidental vessel that delivers eternal spiritual truths. In revealing to the early Hebrews that God created the world, the Holy Spirit descended and accommodated to their knowledge level by using their scientific notions. Our challenge as modern readers of the Bible, then, is to identify this ancient vessel and to separate it from, and not conflate it with, the life-changing Messages of Faith.

Now equipped with some basic terms and definitions, we can examine in detail the various views of origins today. In particular, the impact of scientific concordism on shaping the Christian anti-evolutionary positions will become quite clear.

2

The Spectrum of Origins Positions

MOST PEOPLE TODAY VIEW origins as an evolution vs. creation debate. That is, one is either an "evolutionist" who rejects God, or a "creationist" who believes the world was made in six 24-hour days. Yet some have a dim awareness that this topic is more complex than a simple either/or issue. In a number of churches, Christians are beginning to use the terms young earth creation and old earth creation. The notion of theistic evolution is also appearing, though most view this position as unbiblical and theologically liberal. The terms and definitions introduced in the last chapter make it clear that the origins dichotomy is a false dichotomy. The spectrum of origins positions is much more colorful than the black-and-white positions of atheistic evolution and six-day creation.

This chapter outlines five basic categories of origins: (1) young earth creation, (2) progressive creation, (3) evolutionary creation, (4) deistic evolution, and (5) dysteleological evolution. It is important to underline that beliefs about origins are not limited to only five positions. As you read the chapter, you may find that you hold characteristics from a number of different views. This is perfectly acceptable, and it widens the spectrum of possibilities. The purpose of presenting these categories is to highlight similarities and differences between them, assisting you to make informed choices as you develop your understanding of origins. In order to appreciate fully the various positions, I suggest familiarizing yourself with the table summarizing the different views in Fig 2-1 on page 40 before beginning this chapter.

On a personal note, I have struggled to understand origins for well over twenty years. At various times, I've held the five positions mentioned above in some form or another. Looking back at my voyage, I am amazed at how entrenched I was in the origins dichotomy, and how much I was unaware of it. I was missing a number of vital categories, and as a result, I only had a limited number of choices. Today, it is now clear to me that the origins controversy is rooted in the fact that most people are not fully aware of the different approaches available to them. In other words, this debate is mostly an information problem. Regrettably, our culture and our churches are simply not offering us all the choices. For example, most individuals (like me many years ago) have never even heard of the term evolutionary creation. For those hoping to move beyond the evolution vs. creation debate, the present chapter will explain in more detail this Christian approach to evolution. It is a view of origins that I wish I would have known about soon after I came to Christ.

YOUNG EARTH CREATION

Young earth creation claims that God created the universe and life in six 24-hour days about 6000 years ago. The general public and the Christian community commonly perceive this view of origins to be *the* creationist position. Also known as "creation science" and "scientific creationism," a recent survey of American adults reveals that nearly 90% of born-again Christians believe the world was created in six days and that Gen 1 is "literally true, meaning that it happened that way word-for-word."[1] As a consequence, young earth creationists assert that the early chapters of the Bible offer a reliable scientific record upon which to base research on origins.[2]

According to creation science, God created the world quickly and completely through dramatic, miraculous interventions. This position adamantly rejects cosmological, geological, and biological evolution, insisting that there is no genuine scientific evidence to support these theories. It argues that viewing the physical data in light of a strict literal reading of the biblical creation accounts results in *true* science. For example, young earth creationists claim that fossils and rock layers in the crust of the earth are best explained by Noah's flood. They contend that plants and animals were trapped as these strata were being laid down during a year-long global deluge. Consequently, scientific creationists reject the standard geological dating of rock layers in the 100s of millions of years. Instead, they calculate the world to be around 6000 years old by adding the ages of the individuals recorded in the biblical genealogies. These anti-evolutionists conclude that the presence of scientific facts in the early chapters of Genesis is proof of the supernatural character of Scripture.

Only a God who transcends time could have revealed this information many generations before its discovery by science.

Young earth creation fiercely defends the notion that humanity originates from a single man and woman—literally Adam and Eve as described in Gen 2. This position rejects any connection between the original pair of humans and lower primates because every living species is a separate and special creation. Scientific creationism also contends that pain, decay, and death did not exist in the world before Adam and Eve fell into sin. Their sinful acts in the garden of Eden led to God's judgment upon humanity and the launching of suffering and death on the entire creation. This radical change in the physical world is known as the "cosmic fall."

In order to understand origins, young earth creationists employ a one-way relationship between Scripture and science. The Bible dictates how God created the universe and life, especially how He made humans. At best, scientific discoveries only confirm the events recorded in the biblical creation accounts. In other words, creation science accepts a strict scientific concordism.

The strongest argument for six-day creation is that a literal interpretive approach is the natural and traditional way to read the first chapter of Scripture. This view of origins is undoubtedly closest to that held by the inspired author of Gen 1. Other biblical writers also understood this creation account literally. For example, Moses in recording the Fourth Commandment orders Israel:

> Remember the Sabbath day by keeping it holy. Six days you shall labor and do all your work, but the seventh day is a Sabbath to the Lord your God. On it you shall not do any work, neither you, nor your son or daughter, nor your manservant or maidservant, nor your animals, nor the alien within your gates. *For in six days the Lord made the heavens and the earth, the sea, and all that is in them,* but He rested on the seventh day. Therefore the Lord blessed the Sabbath day and made it holy.

Exodus 20:8–11 (my italics)

Christians throughout history have also upheld the strict literal interpretation of Gen 1. Martin Luther, the father of evangelical Christianity, contended that "Moses spoke in the literal sense, not allegorically or figuratively, that the world with all its creatures was created within six days, as the words read. . . . We know from Moses that the world was not in existence before 6000 years ago."[3]

Powerful evidence for a strict literal reading of the first chapters of the Bible comes from Jesus Himself. In defending the institution of marriage, the Lord argued:

> Haven't you read that at the beginning the Creator "made them male and female," and said, "For this reason a man will leave his father and mother and be united to his wife, and the two will become one flesh." So they are no longer two, but one. Therefore what God has joined together, let man not separate.
>
> Matthew 19:4–6

Clearly, Jesus employed a literal interpretation of the first chapters of Genesis (see also Mark 10:2–9; Luke 11:51, 17:26–27). Like young earth creationists, He appealed to biblical verses regarding the creation of the first humans (Gen 1:27) and the existence of Adam and Eve (Gen 2:24). Scripture features many similar passages, and thus serious consideration must be given to a strict literal interpretive approach.[4] Any Christian accepting a view of origins other than creation science must provide convincing arguments as to why Gen 1 and 2 should not be read literally.

The greatest problem with young earth creation is that it completely contradicts every modern scientific discipline that investigates the origin of the universe and life. There are very few scientists working in the disciplines of cosmology, geology, and biology who accept this anti-evolutionary position. Today, these sciences are practiced in tens of thousands of colleges and universities throughout the world, and according to the scientific community, the evidence for evolution is simply overwhelming.

In order to explain the unwavering acceptance of evolution by modern science, many six-day creationists claim that Satan blinds the mind of hundreds of thousands of scientists.[5] Of course, this controversial opinion certainly raises serious pastoral concerns. It would extend to many Christians who accept evolution as God's method of creation, setting the stage for uncharitable exchanges, and even potential divisions in the church. The demonic deception theory also alienates non-Christian evolutionists. If the Lord created the world through an evolutionary process, and unbelieving scientists see the evidence for this theory in their laboratories every day, then is there any doubt that a stumbling block has been placed between them and the Lord Jesus by young earth creationists (2 Cor 6:2–3)?

I certainly appreciate where six-day creationists are coming from, because twenty-five years ago I ferociously defended this view of origins and believed that evolutionary scientists were deceived by Satan. In fact, I wanted to become a creation scientist in order to attack evolutionists in secular universities. Equipping myself for battle, I entered graduate school in theology to study the opening chapters of the book of Genesis. On registration day in September 1984, I promised in my journal "to declare absolute and pure hell on the 'theory' of evolution." But three years later, I came to the shocking conclusion that the Holy Spirit did not reveal scientific facts in the Bible regarding how the world was actually created. I will share more of my story in the next two chapters and present biblical evidence for why I moved away from young earth creation and scientific concordism.

PROGRESSIVE CREATION

Progressive creation asserts that God created life in sequential stages during the 4.5 billion-year history of earth. Often referred to as "old earth creation" and "day-age theory," this position maintains that the creation days in Gen 1 are periods of 100s of millions of years. It also claims that there is a general alignment between the order of creative events in the Bible and the appearance of the inanimate universe and living organisms discovered by modern science.[6]

According to old earth creationists, the Creator made the galaxies, stars, and planets through cosmological and geological evolution. Beginning with the Big Bang, He ordained and sustained natural processes to create the non-living world. This type of divine action was indirect and subtle, and it is termed *providentialistic*. However, progressive creationists emphatically reject biological evolution. They argue that God miraculously formed basic groups of plants and animals at different points in the distant past through direct and dramatic *interventionistic* action. These anti-evolutionists concede that the originally created groups (known as "created kinds") have modified over time, but this biological variability remains within limits because organisms cannot evolve into entirely different forms of life. Thus, day-age creation accepts micro-evolution (e.g., a dog changing into another variety of dog), but rejects the macro-evolution of fish into amphibians, reptiles into mammals, or primitive primates into humans.

Using a general literalism to read Gen 1, progressive creationists assert that the appearance of living organisms in the Bible aligns with the fossil record. Scripture and geology both reveal that life on earth began with simple forms, and sequentially more complex creatures appeared, until finally humans arrived. These anti-evolutionists also claim that there are huge gaps between fossil groups, and that this reflects God's intermittent interventionist action in the origin of basic groups of organisms "according to their kinds," as recorded in Gen 1. Progressive creationists contend that such a correspondence between the Bible and science testifies to the supernatural character of Scripture, because only a Creator who transcends time could have revealed such information. Lastly, modern geology and general literalism shape the interpretation of Noah's flood for old earth creationists. They maintain that the flood is historical, but it was a local event limited to a region in the Middle East, since the crust of the earth offers no evidence for a global deluge.

Progressive creation firmly defends that humanity arose from a single couple—Adam and Eve as described in Gen 2. Humans are a created kind or basic life group that God made through dramatic interventionistic action. This view of origins fiercely opposes human evolution. However, it acknowledges that the fossil record reveals the physical suffering, decay, and death of living organisms for 100s of millions of years prior to the appearance of humans on earth. Consequently, old earth creation asserts that the sins committed by Adam and Eve in the garden of Eden did not lead to the entrance of physical death into the world, but to *spiritual death*. In other words, this position rejects the traditional belief in a cosmic fall.

Progressive creationists embrace a two-way relationship between Scripture and science in understanding the origin of the universe and life. More specifically, they attempt to harmonize God's Books of Words and Works. For example, the divine creative interventions in Gen 1 and 2 shape their explanation of biological data, in particular that of human origins. At the same time, discoveries in cosmology and geology direct their interpretation of the length of the creation days and the extent of the flood. Old earth creationists, therefore, accept a general scientific concordism.

The strongest argument for the day-age theory is that it provides an approach to the origin of the world that employs both the Bible and modern science. Christians are nourished spiritually every day in their reading of Scripture, and at the same time they enjoy daily the fruits of scientific discovery. Most believers demand that these experiences be neither in conflict nor placed in isolated compartments in their mind. After all, God is the Author of His Words and the Creator of His Works. Moreover, the Lord has given humanity the ability to investigate Scripture and nature.

It is quite reasonable, then, for Christians to assume the existence of a harmony and correspondence between these Two Divine Books. By featuring both a belief in the Bible as the Word of God and an acceptance of the modern sciences of geology and cosmology, old earth creation meets the yearning for a worldview that integrates Christian faith and scientific investigation.

A serious difficulty with progressive creation is that it introduces a false dichotomy between the physical and life sciences. On one hand, it accepts cosmology and geology, including the theory that unites these sciences—the evolution of the inanimate universe. But on the other, it rejects the unifying principle of biological science—the evolution of all living organisms. This position asserts that although galaxies, stars, and planets emerged through natural processes ordained and sustained by God, He did not fully equip the creation for life to arise in a similar manner. However, the scientific method does not distinguish biology from cosmology and geology. All of these sciences are built on the principle that natural processes are dependable, predictable, and even extendable back into the past. Medicine, agriculture, and crime scene investigations are based on the regularity of nature's biological laws in the same way that this notion is used in cosmological and geological studies.

A more serious problem with progressive creation is that it is a God-of-the-gaps model of origins. This position sees divine creative activity in gaps or discontinuities throughout the history of life. Old earth creationists claim that natural processes are insufficient and cannot produce living organisms. Therefore, the Creator's direct intervention is needed to complete a world that He at first created deficient. The difficulty with this understanding of divine action is that when physical processes are discovered to explain a gap once thought to be a site of God's action, His purported intervention vanishes in the advancing light of science. Such a situation raises serious pastoral concerns. If Christians base their faith on the missing fossils between the so-called created kinds, and science eventually discovers them along with the natural mechanisms for evolutionary change, then these believers become vulnerable to losing their faith in Scripture and ultimately the Lord.

The history of science reveals the problem with the God-of-the-gaps. For example, during the 1600s, the famed physicist Sir Isaac Newton claimed that God intervened in order to correct wobbles in the orbits of Saturn and Mercury. He contended that otherwise, these irregularities would eventually lead to the collapse of the solar system. However, this was before the discovery of Uranus and its gravitational pull on Saturn, and prior to the theory of relativity to explain the motion of Mercury. It is also now known that these wobbles are self-correcting. Clearly, Newton's view of divine action in nature was based on an incomplete understanding of astronomy. This trend appears throughout the history of science: as science advances, the gaps always close. And this is the problem with progressive creation. The gaps are not gaps in nature indicative of God's interventionistic action in creating distinct groups of living organisms, but gaps in biological knowledge.

Personally, I have never embraced progressive creation in its fullest sense. During graduate school in theology it became obvious to me that the Bible does not reveal scientific facts about origins, and therefore aligning the days of Genesis with modern science is not possible. If anything, I became a muddled progressive creationist by default, because I was no longer a young earth creationist and I fervently continued to reject evolution. But why did I remain an anti-evolutionist? Well, to use the blunt words of a scientist visiting my science-religion class, "Denis, you just don't know enough about evolution." Needless to say, I was hopping mad when I was told this in front of my classmates. Yet looking back now, the professor did have an excellent point, and I believe the Holy Spirit was talking to me through him. My training in science was fairly limited. Most of my education to that point was in dentistry, not the evolutionary sciences. In other words, there was a huge gap in my biological knowledge and I used a God-of-the-gaps approach to explain things I did not understand, like the origin of life. However, that changed after I entered a PhD program in biology with a focus on evolution. By God's grace, large gaps in my knowledge began to close. I will share more of my story in chapter 5.

EVOLUTIONARY CREATION

Evolutionary creation asserts that God created the universe and life through an ordained, sustained, and design-reflecting evolutionary process. This position fully embraces both the religious beliefs of biblical Christianity and the scientific theories of cosmological, geological, and biological evolution. It contends that the Creator established and maintains the laws of nature, including the mechanisms of a teleological evolution. Notably, this view of origins argues that humanity evolved from pre-human ancestors, and through this process the Image of God and human sin were gradually and mysteriously manifested. Evolutionary creationists experience God's love and presence in their lives, and they enjoy a personal relationship with the Lord Jesus that includes miraculous signs and wonders.[7]

The category evolutionary creation might seem like a contradiction in terms. This indeed would be the case if the words evolution and creation were restricted to their popular meanings. That is, if the former is conflated with a dysteleological worldview, and if the latter refers exclusively to young earth creation. But this Christian approach to evolution employs professional definitions and moves beyond the evolution vs. creation dichotomy. The most important word in this category is the noun creation. Evolutionary creationists are first and foremost thoroughly committed and unapologetic creationists. They believe that the universe is a creation that is absolutely dependent for its every instant of existence on the will and grace of the Creator. The qualifying word in this category is the adjective evolutionary, indicating the method through which God created the world. This view of origins is often referred to as "theistic evolution." However, that word arrangement places the process of evolution as the primary term, and makes the Creator secondary as only a qualifying adjective. Such an inversion in priority is unacceptable to me and other evolutionary creationists.

Another reason for the category evolutionary creation is that the word theistic carries such a wide variety of meanings today. Derived from *theos*, the common Greek word for god, the proper definition of theism refers to a personal god, like the God of Christianity. But as everyone knows, there are countless numbers of different gods. Therefore, the term evolutionary creation distinguishes conservative Christians who love Jesus and accept evolution from the evolutionary interpretations of deists (belief in the impersonal god-of-the-philosophers), pantheists (everything in the universe is god), panentheists (the world is god's body and god is the world's mind/soul), new-age pagans (god is a divine force or entity in nature), and liberal Christians (Jesus is only an enlightened human who never rose physically from the dead).

In order to explain their origins position, evolutionary creationists begin by pointing out the remarkable parallels between evolution and human embryological development in the womb. They argue that God's action in the creation of each person individually is similar to His activity in the origin of the entire world collectively. Four analogous features include:

First, embryological and evolutionary processes are both teleological and ordained by God. At conception, the DNA in a fertilized human egg is fully equipped with the necessary information for a person to develop during the nine months of pregnancy. Similarly, the Creator loaded into the Big Bang the plan and capability for the universe and life, including humans, to evolve over 10–15 billion years.

Second, divine creative action in the origin of individual humans and the entire world is through sustained and continuous natural processes. That is, it is providentialistic, and not interventionistic. No Christian believes that while in his or her mother's womb the Lord came out of heaven and dramatically intervened to attach a nose, set an eye, or bore an ear canal. Rather, everyone understands embryological development to be an uninterrupted natural process that God subtly maintains during pregnancy. In the same way, evolutionary creationists assert that dramatic divine interventions (God-of-the-gaps miracles) were not employed in the creation of the cosmos and living organisms, including people. Instead, evolution is an unbroken natural process that the Lord sustained throughout eons of time.

Third, human embryological development in the microcosm of the womb and evolution in the macrocosm of the world reflect intelligent design. That is, each is a natural revelation authored by the Creator. The psalmist praises his Maker, "For You created my inmost being; You knit me together in my mother's womb. I praise You because I am fearfully and wonderfully made" (Ps 139:13–14). Similarly, evolutionary creationists view evolution as a "knitting" process that results in a world that is "fearfully and wonderfully made." Indeed, the Big Bang "declares the Glory of God," and biological evolution "proclaims the work of His hands" (Ps 19:1).

Finally, spiritual mysteries are associated with both the embryological and evolutionary processes that created humans. Men and women are utterly unique and distinguished from the rest of creation because only they bear the Image of God and have fallen into sin. Christians throughout the ages have debated where, when, and how these spiritual realities are manifested in the development of each individual. Yet history reveals that the church has not come to a consensus on these questions, implying that these issues are beyond human understanding. In other words, they are mysteries. Similarly, evolutionary creationists believe that the manifestation of God's Image and the entrance of sin into the world during human evolution are also a mystery. Christian evolutionists firmly accept these spiritual realities, but recognize that understanding their origin completely is beyond our creaturely capacity to know.

Evolutionary creation is built on the Two Divine Books model—the Creator reveals Himself both through Scripture and science. In the Book of God's Words, He specifically discloses His character and will for the world. The Bible is the revelation of Jesus Christ and His amazing love for humanity. Scripture leads men and women into a genuine relationship with the Lord through the confession of their sins and the acceptance of forgiveness through His sacrifice on the Cross. The Word also offers the principles for a holy life. As the apostle Paul states, "All Scripture is God-breathed and is useful for teaching, rebuking, correcting, and training in righteousness so that the man and woman of God may be thoroughly equipped for every good work" (2 Tim 3:16–17).

Regarding the opening chapters of the Bible, evolutionary creation asserts that Gen 1–3 is an ancient origins account inspired by the Holy Spirit. First and foremost, it reveals a Divine Theology that includes foundations of the Christian faith: (1) God created the world, (2) the creation is very good, (3) humans are the only creatures made in the Image of God, (4) every man and woman has fallen into sin, and (5) God judges humanity for their sinful acts. These are Messages of Faith that change lives and upon which joyous and successful lives are built.

In order to reveal these spiritual truths as effectively as possible to the ancient biblical authors and their readers, evolutionary creationists contend that the Holy Spirit accommodated and employed the science-of-the-day. For example, Scripture features a 3-tier universe with heaven above, the earth in the middle, and the underworld below (Fig 3-2; p. 47). Ancient science is therefore a vehicle that transports Messages of Faith. The opening chapters of Genesis also include ancient poetry. Of course, the term poetry carries a number of meanings. But using the most basic definition, it refers simply to a structured writing style in contrast to a free flowing narrative. To illustrate, the Gen 1 creation account is built on parallel panels (Fig 4-2; p. 74). Most would agree that actual events in the past do not unfold in such a structured fashion. Evolutionary creationists conclude that the purpose of Gen 1–3 is to reveal inerrant spiritual truths, and not the details of modern science ahead of time.

Evolutionary creation also asserts that the Book of God's Works reveals the Creator. He has gifted us with marvelous minds and the ability to investigate the natural world. Through science, we can think God's thoughts after Him and discover His method of creating the universe and life. According to this position, the physical evidence for cosmological, geological, and biological evolution is *overwhelming*. In addition, science contributes to seeing the non-verbal natural revelation of the Creator's glory, power, and divine nature. History demonstrates that the deeper scientists probe nature with telescopes or microscopes, greater and more magnificent pictures of His majesty emerge. Evolutionary creationists are quick to point out that they have an expanded and more robust understanding of intelligent design than the anti-evolutionists. Christian evolutionists not only affirm design in the present structures and operations of the creation, they also recognize reflections of intelligence in the mechanisms of evolution.

Therefore, evolutionary creation embraces a complementary relationship between Scripture and science in understanding origins.[8] Together they fulfill each other; alone they are incomplete. Scientific discoveries reveal *how* the Creator made this spectacular design-reflecting world, while the Bible declares precisely *who* created it—the God of Christianity. More precisely, evolutionary creation accepts theological concordism, but rejects scientific concordism.

The most compelling argument for evolutionary creation is that it embraces without any reservations both biblical faith and modern science. Like a breath of fresh air, this position moves beyond the stagnant origins dichotomy and the science-religion warfare myth, both of which have imprisoned many minds throughout most of the twentieth century. Evolutionary creation meets the yearning of a scientific generation in search of spiritual meaning. In particular, it offers an intellectually satisfying worldview for those who experience God in a personal relationship and know His creation through science. Though this position recognizes that science and religion operate within their respective domains, it does not suffer from the intellectual schizophrenia of placing them in isolated compartments. Rather, many areas of common interest exist, including bioethics, the soul and mind-brain problem, and intelligent design in nature. In dealing with such issues, evolutionary creationists enjoy a respectful and fruitful dialogue between the best modern science and the foundations of biblical Christianity.

Evolutionary creation is the only Christian view of origins that offers a unified vision of science. This position does not postulate that certain scientific disciplines are logically flawed or spiritually deceived. There is no discrimination between sciences dealing with the daily operation of the world and those investigating its past origins. And it does not segregate evolutionary biology from cosmology and geology. For example, young earth creation has a disjointed understanding of science. On the one hand, it rejects the evolutionary sciences. Yet on the other hand, these anti-evolutionists support and even practice modern engineering and medical sciences, accepting research built on the assumption that natural processes feature robust regularity. Similarly, progressive creation has a double standard in its science. It affirms the evolution of the inanimate universe as offered by cosmological and geological sciences, but it dismisses the unifying principle of biological science that life evolved. Evolutionary creationists reject these false dichotomies and uphold the unity and coherence of all the natural sciences, because they are ultimately rooted in God. In fact, Christian evolutionists believe that every scientific discipline is a gift from the Lord.

The greatest problem with evolutionary creation is that it does not embrace the traditional literal interpretation of the opening chapters of the Bible. Church history shows that nearly all Christians have understood Gen 1–3 to be a basic record of actual events in the past. Specifically, most have believed that Gen 2 reveals that human history began with Adam and Eve. More troubling for this evolutionary position is the fact that Jesus and the biblical authors often refer to the early chapters of Genesis as a literal historical account. And the most acute difficulty is explaining the relationship between human sin and the origin of physical death. Genesis 3, Rom 5 and 8, and 1 Cor 15 clearly state that death came into the world after the creation of Adam and his original sin. Yet this Christian view of evolution asserts that the fossil record conclusively demonstrates that death existed for 100s of millions of years prior to the appearance of humans (Fig 4-3; p. 84). In other words, evolutionary creation rejects the traditional Christian belief in the cosmic fall.

Consequently, evolutionary creationists contend that the biblical accounts of origins must be read in a very unnatural and counterintuitive way. They suggest that Christians need to move beyond scientific concordism and the traditional literal approach that has marked the interpretation of these chapters throughout history. However, before any believer considers accepting evolutionary creation, the problems cited above regarding Gen 1–3, Rom 5 and 8, and 1 Cor 15 need to be addressed directly. I will attempt to offer some solutions in chapter six.

Evolutionary creation is the view of origins I hold today. But I only came to this position after ten years of graduate school study at the PhD level in both theology and biology. I then spent another ten years working out the implications of this Christian view of origins. Admittedly, it is not an easy position to accept. My working assumption throughout this period was that God is the Creator of the world and the Author of the Bible. I certainly saw conflicts and contradictions between the Two Divine Books, but I trusted in the Lord and I believed that there *had* to be a solution. The most important discovery during my journey was recognizing that there was ancient science in Scripture. Once freed from scientific concordism, I was allowed to let the scientific evidence lead me to wherever it went—and it led me to the conclusion that Jesus created the world through evolution.

DEISTIC EVOLUTION

Deistic evolution asserts that god initiated the evolutionary process and then retreated from the universe, never to return. This position depicts the creator as one who winds the cosmos like a clock, and then lets it run down on its own without any interference. In contrast to biblical Christianity, the supreme being of deism is impersonal. Often called the god-of-the-philosophers, the deistic creator is not involved in the lives of men and women. This god never reveals himself personally through scriptures, prayer, or miracles. He simply does not seem to care about us. Regrettably, many miscategorize this view as theistic evolution, but as noted earlier, the term theism refers to a personal God. In many ways, deistic evolution characterizes liberal Christianity, since it spurns belief in divine action and biblical revelation. Clearly, deistic evolution is radically different from evolutionary creation.

According to deistic evolutionists, god loosely ordained natural laws through which the universe and life evolved, but he did not remain in the world to sustain these physical processes. Deists claim that his only creative act was to set off the Big Bang, 10–15 billion years ago. Notably, this position asserts that modern cosmology presents physical data for intelligent design, pointing to the mind of a divine being. However, it contends that nature is a closed continuum of mechanical processes only. By pushing the creator outside the universe, deists deem notions such as the Holy Spirit inspiring prophets, or God becoming a man in the person of Jesus, to be ancient superstitions. Thus, they firmly reject biblical revelation. These evolutionists argue that since Scripture contains the beliefs of ignorant ancient peoples, it has little to no value for our scientific generation.

Deistic evolution asserts that humanity evolved from ancient primates. There is debate as to whether the creator specifically intended the present human species to evolve, or whether the evolutionary process was ordained only to produce some form of intelligent life. In other words, there is no consensus on the ultimate status of humanity. But this position definitely rejects the creation of a literal Adam and Eve as described in Gen 2. And it dismisses the foundational biblical principles that men and women bear the Image of God and have fallen into sin.

In order to understand origins, deistic evolutionists claim that there is no relationship between Scripture and science. Though they embrace the non-verbal natural revelation of intelligent design in the Book of God's Works, they spurn the special, verbal revelation of the Lord's love for humanity as disclosed in the Book of God's Words. Deistic evolutionists believe that Gen 1–3 is an irrelevant origins myth. As a consequence, they reject both theological and scientific concordism.

The problem with deistic evolution is that a god who winds the clock of the universe and then leaves it to run down on its own rarely meets anyone's spiritual needs. An impersonal designer may titillate the intellectual curiosity of some for a brief period, but such a distant being is, for all practical purposes, irrelevant and non-existent. As history reveals, deism was popular in Europe during the 1700s, but most eventually realized that an absentee designer is superfluous and dispensable. Only a century after his birth, the god of deism died from public view and was buried in the grave of private thoughts and personal beliefs where he remains today. In contrast to Christianity, deism never inspired an enduring body of believers, an educational institution, or an outreach facility like a hospital or food bank. Religious beliefs restricted to logical arguments for the existence of god, like the argument from design, leave most people cold and seldom inspire anyone to personal commitment and involvement. The gospel of deism rarely, if ever, transforms lives in the way that the gospel of Jesus Christ throughout history has led men and women to be born again.

Another difficulty with deistic evolution is that it fails to appreciate the limits of human thinking. Deism began to emerge after the birth of modern science. The dramatic success of the scientific method led to a flagrant optimism in human rationality. In effect, deists made reason an idol, and this blind faith led many to assume that the principles of morality, the mysteries of life, and the knowledge of god could be worked out within their mind. However, history reveals the failure of deism—ethical consensus does not exist, mysteries remain unexplained, and theological agreement has never emerged. This position fails to understand that human reason is a creaturely rationality with boundaries defined by the God of the Bible. As the apostle Paul states, "We know in part" and "now we see but a poor reflection" (1 Cor 13:9, 12). In addition, deists do not recognize the reality of sin and its impact on the human mind. According to Paul, idolatry causes thinking to become "futile" and even "depraved" (Rom 1:21, 28). In a subtle way, deism points to the necessity of an authoritative divine revelation like the Bible, which transcends the intellectual limits and sinful tendencies of human reason.

I entered college in 1972, and by the end of my freshman year I was basically a deist. Entrenched in the origins dichotomy, a biology course on evolution in the fall term completely destroyed my belief in the Bible and organized religion. I had no idea that there was a religiously and scientifically rigorous view of origins like evolutionary creation. Though I did not reject the existence of God outright, I lived as if He did not exist. Except, of course, when I desperately needed Him, like when it looked as if I might become a teenage father. I sure prayed a lot then. In other words, I was a deist with a god-of-the-emergencies to save me from the consequences of my foolishness and immorality. But every time potentially disastrous situations passed, I hypocritically returned to the 1970s lifestyle of the drugs, sex, and rock n' roll generation.

DYSTELEOLOGICAL EVOLUTION

Dysteleological evolution states that the universe and life evolved only by blind chance and without any plan or purpose whatsoever. In such a world, there is no God and no ultimate right or wrong. It is marked by utter meaninglessness. Often using the expression "nothing but," dysteleologists believe that we are nothing but molecules. This position is also referred to as scientism, atheistic evolution, and scientific materialism. Regrettably, it is also called Darwinism, even though Charles Darwin, near the end of his life, explicitly stated that he was never an atheist.[9] Regarding ethics and morality, dysteleological evolutionists embrace humanism. That is, they place themselves in the position of God and then determine right and wrong. Under the controlling influence of the media and secular education, this view of origins has spread throughout our culture. Consequently, the general public and the church commonly perceive dysteleological evolution to be *the* evolutionist position as well as that held by the scientific community.[10]

Atheists reject the existence of God. They believe that matter and energy are the only realities in the universe. Dysteleologists arrive at this conclusion through a *personal commitment* to the belief that science is the only method for determining truth, and that the scientific method can reduce everything into nothing but molecules. Therefore, all non-scientific forms of knowledge, like religion, are deemed utterly irrelevant. Atheists contend that religious behavior is an evolutionary by-product that arose by chance and contributed to the survival of the human herd. This position therefore rejects natural revelation. Moral intuition, the reflection of intelligent design, and the sense that the world has an ultimate purpose are said to be nothing but delusions that have evolved in the human mind. Dysteleological evolution also dismisses biblical revelation. It contends that the authors of Scripture wrote under the influence of a pre-scientific mindset, which led to the belief that the universe is filled with supernatural activity. From this perspective, the miracles in the Bible, including the Incarnation and the bodily resurrection of Jesus, are spurned as fantasies concocted by human imagination and wishful thinking.

Dysteleological evolution claims that humanity evolved from ancient primates entirely through blind chance and random natural processes. That is, humans are nothing but an unintended spin-off of biological evolution without any ultimate purpose. This position vehemently rejects the creation of a literal Adam and Eve as stated in Gen 2, and fiercely dismisses the biblical notions that men and women bear the Image of God and have fallen into sin. Instead, atheistic evolutionists assert that sin is only a relative cultural relic, and that humanity has created God in its image.

In order to understand origins, dysteleological evolutionists defend a one-way relationship between Scripture and science. They reduce God and religion into nothing but biological and sociological phenomena. Dysteleologists claim that scientific evidence not only determines *how* the world originated, but it even explains *why* there is no ultimate purpose in the cosmos. According to this position, Gen 1–3 is only a pre-scientific myth about the beginning of the world, and it has no relevance whatsoever for us today. Atheistic evolutionists adamantly reject both theological and scientific concordism.

The greatest problem with dysteleological evolution is that it flies directly in the face of God and the First Commandment: "You shall have no other gods before Me" (Exod 20:3; Deut 5:7). This position commits the greatest of all sins: atheists place themselves before God! They fashion a worldview that relegates their Maker to the realm of delusion. The creature in essence takes the place of the Creator. But if God and the spiritual realm exist, then dysteleological evolution is not only the most nauseating act of arrogance in intellectual history, but it is also an understanding of the world that is hopelessly flawed, because it lacks the foundation of reality and knowledge—the Maker of heaven and earth. Scripture calls those who do not acknowledge the Creator fools. Twice in the Psalms it is written, "The fool says in his heart, 'There is no God'" (14:1, 53:1). The Proverbs also state that "fools hate knowledge" (1:22, 29) and that "fools mock at making amends for sin" (14:9). Atheistic evolutionists reject the existence of God, construct a worldview without reference to Him, and dismiss sin as irrelevant. In light of God's Word, dysteleological evolution is the origins position of fools.*

Another serious difficulty with dysteleological evolution is that it is a *personal commitment* to the belief that truth is only found through scientific investigation. This view of knowledge is known as positivism and reductionism. It asserts that all phenomena, including religious experience, can be reduced by science into nothing but simple physical laws. Ironically, atheists fail to recognize that there is no scientific test or experiment to prove this claim. They put their *faith* in the methods of science in a way similar to religious people who embrace belief in God. But even more troubling is the fact that this view of origins *trusts* the human brain, an organ that supposedly evolved merely by blind chance and that was never intended to discover truth. In a dysteleological world, the

---

* A qualification needs to be made regarding what may appear to be a harsh judgment against dysteleological evolutionists and a betrayal of my insistence that respect characterize discussions about origins. I make no apology for what the Bible clearly states—atheists are fools. Of course, the term fool is controversial since today it means being stupid, idiotic, etc. But the biblical notion of knowledge is holistic, integrating seamlessly facts and godly wisdom. A person, then, could be brilliant in determining scientific facts (which atheists do very well), but at the same time, because of sin, a complete failure in recognizing the religious implications of this data. Thus, foolishness is tied directly to sinfulness and the rejection of the greatest of all commandments: To love God with all our heart, soul, strength and *mind* (Matt 22:37; Mark 12:30; Luke 10:27).

brain would have arisen for the sole purposes of fighting, fleeing, feeding, and "fertilizing." But how can an organ fashioned by irrational processes make true statements about ultimate reality? Why should atheists *believe* in such claims worked out in their brain? It is clear that dysteleological belief is contradictory and self-referentially incoherent.

Finally, atheistic evolution fails to meet the spiritual and psychological needs of most men and women. Few throughout history have espoused this bleak worldview marked by ultimate purposelessness, meaninglessness, and hopelessness. One study reveals that about 95% of Americans believe in the existence of God or a universal spirit.[11] In other words, at best only 5% of the general population hold dysteleological beliefs. Moreover, atheistic evolution renders human experience psychologically empty. For example, the reductionist method concludes that love is *nothing but* a manifestation of biochemical activity in the brain. Accordingly, the notion of love is ultimately a delusion imposed on human relationships for the survival of the species. But does anyone who is in love believe that? Is a good marriage merely a herd response? No. Love is *something more* than just chemicals in our head. It is a spiritual reality ordained by the God of love that is beyond scientific detection, and it is known only through the "instrument" of the human heart.

The deism of my early college years slipped in and out of agnostic periods until finally I embraced atheism and a dysteleological view of evolution. In a journal entry in 1977 during my last year of dentistry school, I came to the conclusion that "love is a protective response characteristic of all animals, except expressed to greater levels in man because of his superior intelligence." I remember when I wrote this. I was wickedly cynical at the time. One of my favorite sayings was "love is nothing but a herd response." In other words, humans are just a herd of mating animals. It does not take much imagination to envision how I treated women. Even marriage didn't really mean anything because it was nothing but a social convention invented by men to control society. There wasn't anything sacred about it, since after all, the Sacred did not exist. Though my heart was hardening and getting darker, there was still a small voice telling me that my godless lifestyle was wrong. Today, I now realize that this is the moral law that God has written on each and every human heart to save us from our foolishness (Rom 2:14–15).

RELATIONSHIPS BETWEEN THE ORIGINS POSITIONS

Fig 2-1 outlines the five basic positions on the origin of the universe and life. This table reveals that the evolution vs. creation debate is a false dichotomy. Four of the positions believe that the world is the creation of God (young earth creation, progressive creation, evolutionary creation, deistic evolution), and three accept that living organisms arose through evolution (evolutionary creation, deistic evolution, dysteleological evolution). In other words, there are four types of creationists and three types of evolutionists. I believe, then, that the time has come for everyone to move beyond the simplistic either/or approach to origins.

It is important to emphasize that Fig 2-1 is an instructional framework with limits. This table assists in organizing the spectrum of origins positions. In the same way that five basic categories of color (red, orange, yellow, green, blue) can be used to describe a rainbow with its incalculable shades and hues, the chart does not offer every possible view of origins. For example, two other positions could have been included: (1) evolutionary religious agnostics—individuals who accept evolution but do not know if God exists; and (2) Christian scientific agnostics—believers who do not know if the scientific evidence supports evolution because they are not educated in cosmology, geology, or biology (e.g., lawyers, engineers, philosophers, etc.). If readers find that their view of origins includes features from different categories in the table, this is perfectly acceptable. It widens the spectrum of positions and offers more evidence that the origins dichotomy is a false dichotomy.

Fig 2-1 presents a few notable features. First and foremost, the conservative Christian origins positions are united by the redeeming Blood of Jesus Christ and the hope of eternal life. Young earth creation, progressive creation, and evolutionary creation also share foundational Christian beliefs in: the creation of the world by the God of the Bible, intelligent design in nature, personal divine action, the inspiration of Scripture by the Holy Spirit, every human bearing the Image of God, the sinfulness of all human beings, and biblical ethics. Anyone who knows the Lord personally will agree that these are basic spiritual truths of their faith. Church history also reveals that these inerrant theological principles have formed the core of creeds and doctrines throughout the ages. Christians in the origins debate today stand united in affirming the creatorship and lordship of the God of the Bible.

Second, scientific concordism in Gen 1–3 is the central factor that leads to differences between the conservative Christian views of origins. Young earth creationists reject cosmological, geological, and biological evolution, arguing that these sciences are unbiblical. In harmonizing Gen 1 and scientific evidence, progressive creationists accept the first two sciences mentioned, but dismiss the last because this creation account states that living organisms were made "according to their kinds." Evolutionary creationists embrace fully the three modern evolutionary sciences and completely reject scientific concordism. Regarding divine action in the origin of the world, creation scientists claim that God used dramatic interventions as revealed in Gen 1. Day-age creationists assert that life appeared by direct miraculous acts, while the inanimate world arose indirectly through natural processes. Christian evolutionists reject dramatic miracles in origins. They argue that Scripture does not reveal God's creative method. *However, logic dictates that the views of two of these three Christian origins positions are wrong.* This being the case, a serious pastoral and pedagogical consequence exists: error is being preached and taught within our churches and Christian schools. Consequently, determining the truthfulness or falsity of scientific concordism in Gen 1–3 is a critical issue for us today. The next two chapters will focus on whether or not the Holy Spirit revealed scientific facts in Scripture.

Finally, the box outlined at the center of Fig 2-1 is the key to understanding divine action from an evolutionary creationist perspective. Christian evolutionists assert that God created the world indirectly through ordained and sustained evolutionary processes, and that the Creator acts both dramatically and subtly in the lives of people through miracles, signs, and wonders. The lines in the lower middle column of Fig 2-1 through "Interpretation of Genesis 1–3" and "Concordism in Genesis 1–3" are pivotal in understanding these early chapters of Scripture. Evolutionary creationists conclude that the purpose of the Bible is to reveal God and inerrant spiritual truths, and not how He actually created the world and humanity.

Clearly, there are differences among conservative Christians over the issue of origins, and the potential exists for divisions to arise in the Body of Jesus. The apostle Paul offers insight and perspective that is applicable to this situation today. He admonishes that divisions should never appear in the church and that our focus should always be on Christ (1 Cor 1:10–13). Details about how the Lord made the world or how He revealed

	YOUNG EARTH CREATION The "Creationist" Position 6-Day Creation	PROGRESSIVE CREATION Old Earth Creation Day-Age Theory
Teleology	Yes	Yes
Intelligent Design	Yes Points to a Designer	Yes Points to a Designer
Age of the Universe	Young 6000 years	Old 10-15 billion years
Evolution of Life	Rejects macro-evolution Accepts micro-evolution	Rejects macro-evolution Accepts micro-evolution
God's Activity in the Origin of the Universe & Life	Yes Direct Interventions over 6 days	Yes 1. Direct for basic "kinds" of life Interventions over billions of yrs 2. Indirect for inanimate universe Ordained & sustained natural processes
God's Activity in the Lives of Men & Women	Yes Personal God Dramatic & subtle	Yes Personal God Dramatic & subtle
Nature of the Bible	Word of God Inspired by Holy Spirit	Word of God Inspired by Holy Spirit
Interpretation of Genesis 1-3	Strict literalism Creation days = 24 hrs Global flood	General literalism Creation days = Geologic ages Local flood

Concordism
in Genesis 1-3
  Theological
  Scientific
	
	Yes
	Yes
		
		Yes
		Yes

Origin of Humanity	Adam & Eve Accepts Image of God Accepts sin	Adam & Eve Accepts Image of God Accepts sin
Theology/Philosophy	Conservative Christianity	Conservative Christianity
Ethics	Biblical	Biblical

Fig 2-1. Positions on the Origin of the Universe and Life. The lines and box indicate categorical features that are critical to understanding evolutionary creation. See text for explanation.

EVOLUTIONARY CREATION Theistic Evolution	DEISTIC EVOLUTION God-of-the-Philosophers "Theistic" Evolution	DYSTELEOLOGICAL EVOLUTION The "Evolutionist" Position Atheistic Evolution
Yes	Yes	No Plan & purpose a delusion
Yes Points to a Designer	Yes Points to a Designer	No Design a delusion
Old 10-15 billion years	Old 10-15 billion years	Old 10-15 billion years
Accepts macro-evolution Accepts micro-evolution	Accepts macro-evolution Accepts micro-evolution	Accepts macro-evolution Accepts micro-evolution
Yes Indirect Ordained & sustained natural processes	Yes Indirect Ordained natural processes God never enters the world	No Nothing but blind chance natural processes God a delusion
Yes Personal God Dramatic & subtle	No Impersonal God God never enters the world	No No God God a delusion
Word of God Inspired by Holy Spirit	Human superstitions Rejects divine revelation God never enters the world	Human superstitions Rejects divine revelation God a delusion
1. Divine Theology 2. Ancient science 3. Ancient poetry	Irrelevant origins myth	Irrelevant origins myth
Yes No	No No	No No
Humanity evolved Accepts Image of God Accepts sin	Humanity evolved Rejects Image of God Rejects sin	Humanity evolved Rejects Image of God Rejects sin
Conservative Christianity	Deism & Liberal Christianity	Atheism
Biblical	Humanism	Humanism

Messages of Faith in Gen 1–3 must not tear believers apart. Instead, through respectful dialogue, Christians with different views about origins have an opportunity to learn from one another in order to understand more fully the Books of God's Words and Works.

3

Ancient Science in the Bible

THE BIBLE IS A precious gift given to us in order to reveal God and His will. Contained within its pages are the foundations of the Christian faith—the creation of the world, the fall of humanity into sin, the offer of redemption through the Blood shed on the Cross, and the promise of eternal life. The Scriptures are also an everlasting source of spiritual nourishment for our soul. Through the power of the Holy Spirit, the Bible assures and encourages, challenges and admonishes, and equips men and women for a faithful life of good works. Most importantly, the primary purpose of God's Word is to reveal Jesus and the Father's unfathomable love for all of us.

Church history shows us that Christians have not only consulted Scripture for spiritual matters, but have also used it in order to understand the structure, operation, and origin of the world. Scientific concordism has been a prominent feature in theological discussions throughout the ages. As noted previously, the belief that there is an accord or correspondence between the Bible and science is a very reasonable expectation, since God is both the Author of His Words and the Creator of His Works. But the questions must be asked: Is scientific concordism true? Does the science in Scripture actually align with modern scientific evidence? And if scientific concordism is false, does this undermine the Christian faith?

Personally, I completely appreciate and understand Christians who are scientific concordists. They love Scripture and they have a wonderful faith. In fact, I fiercely defended scientific concordism for nearly ten years. When I came to Christ, it was through reading the gospel of John as a literal account of actual events, and the spiritual messages changed my life forever. It made perfect sense then to use this same literal approach with the accounts of origins in the book of Genesis. Consequently, I soon became a young earth creationist. But please note: God descended to my level and met me where I happened to be at that point in my life—an atheist trapped in the origins dichotomy. To me, being a Christian meant rejecting evolution and accepting a literal reading of Gen 1–3. At that time, my university education was limited to dentistry, and I did not have any training in reading the biblical origins accounts. However, this speaks of the amazing power of the Word of God. You do not need a specialized education in theology to know Jesus. You just need to get down on your knees and open Scripture, and you will meet the Lord.

God eventually called me to graduate school in theology, and it was quite a shock, to say the least. My love for Jesus never changed one little bit, but my knowledge of statements about the physical world in Scripture changed dramatically. The best way to introduce this interpretive approach is to consider the Lord's parable of the mustard seed. He asked His disciples:

> With what can we compare the kingdom of God, or what parable will we use for it? It is like a mustard seed, which, when sown upon the ground, is *the smallest of all the seeds on the earth*; yet it grows up and becomes the greatest of all shrubs, and puts forth large branches, so that the birds of the air can make nests in its shade.
>
> Mark 4:30–32 (my italics)[1]

As everyone knows, the mustard seed is not "the smallest of all seeds on the earth." Orchid seeds are much smaller, to cite just one example. Yet perceived through the eyes of ancient people in the Lord's day, mustard seeds were the smallest seeds. That is, from their point of view, or better, from their *ancient phenomenological perspective* (Greek *phainōmenon*: appearance), this was a scientific fact for them. Of course, most Christians understand that Jesus' purpose in this parable is not to teach botany. Rather, He uses the science-of-the-day in order to reveal an inerrant prophecy about the kingdom of God. In other words, the Lord descended and accommodated to the level of His ancient listeners.

Fig 3-1 presents the Message-Incident Principle for the interpretation of biblical passages that refer to the physical world. This approach contends that in order to reveal spiritual truths as effectively as possible to ancient people, the Holy Spirit employed their understanding of nature, which was based on an ancient phenomenological perspective. Instead of confusing or distracting the biblical writers and their readers with modern scientific concepts, God came down to their level and used the science-

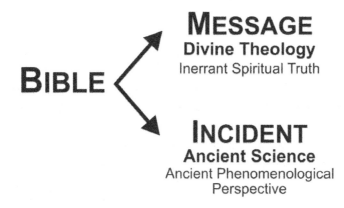

Fig 3-1. The Message-Incident Principle

of-their-day. This is exactly what Jesus did in the mustard seed parable. Therefore, passages in Scripture that deal with the physical world feature both a *Message of Faith* and an *incidental ancient science*. According to this interpretive principle, biblical inerrancy rests in Divine Theology, and not in statements referring to nature. Qualifying ancient science as "incidental" does not mean that it is unimportant. The science in Scripture is vital for transporting the spiritual truths. It acts as a cup or vessel that delivers "living waters" (John 4:10). However, the word incidental carries meanings of "that which happens to be alongside" and "happening in connection with something more important." In other words, the ancient science in Scripture is "alongside" the "more important" Message of Faith.

This chapter embraces the following assumption: As the Word of God judges our thoughts and remodels our mind (Heb 4:12; Rom 12:1–2), features like the ancient science in Scripture help us to evaluate and reshape our view of how the Holy Spirit revealed through the inspired biblical writers. By using an inductive Bible study method, I will offer evidence that an ancient phenomenological perspective of the structure and operation of the physical world appears throughout Scripture. The presence of ancient science certainly has significant implications, especially for the origins debate. If the Word of God features an ancient view of nature, then the popular Christian belief in scientific concordism must be reconsidered. Stated more precisely, if there is an ancient science regarding the structure and operation of the world, then consistency argues that there is also an ancient science of origins. Should this be the case, we would need to re-think our use of the Bible in understanding how God actually created the universe and life.

READING SCRIPTURE THROUGH ANCIENT EYES

A simple thought experiment introduces the challenge of interpreting biblical passages that refer to the physical world. Consider the first two verses of Scripture, and then envision the scene that is described. Genesis 1:1–2 states, "In the beginning God created the heavens and the earth. Now the earth was formless and empty, darkness was over the surface of the deep, and the Spirit of God was hovering over the waters." Most people picture a dark, watery, and chaotic setting that features a *spherical* earth. That is, when reading the word "earth," they automatically envision a globe. But is this the biblical understanding of the earth's structure? Or are people reading their twenty-first century science *into* the Bible, rather than allowing God's Word to speak for itself? A few facts from Scripture answer these questions.

First, the use of the word earth in the Bible indicates that the Holy Spirit did not intend to reveal modern scientific information about the structure of the world. It appears about 2500 times in the Old Testament (*'eres*) and 250 times in the New Testament (*gē*).[2] Never once is the earth referred to as spherical. Nor is a spherical shape implied by the context of any passage.* Indeed, if it was God's purpose to reveal in Scripture the scientific fact that the earth is a sphere, then there were 2750 opportunities to do so. He could easily have done this by comparing the earth to something round, like a ball or an orange. Surely, if it were the Lord's intention to reveal science in the Bible, then we would expect Him to tell us something about the structure of the home that He made for us. But He never did. This scriptural evidence argues that scientific concordism was not the goal of the Holy Spirit in biblical revelation.

Second, to the surprise of most Christians, the Bible presents a 3-tiered universe, indicating that the inspired ancient authors believed the earth was flat. One of the most important passages in the New Testament is the Kenotic Hymn (Greek *kenoō*: to empty, pour out), and it features this view of the structure of the cosmos. Highlighting the fact that God emptied Himself and came down to the level of humans in the person of Jesus, the apostle Paul writes:

---

* Some readers might be quick to argue that Job 26:7 and Isa 40:22 imply that the earth is spherical. These verses are dealt with later in the chapter on p. 63.

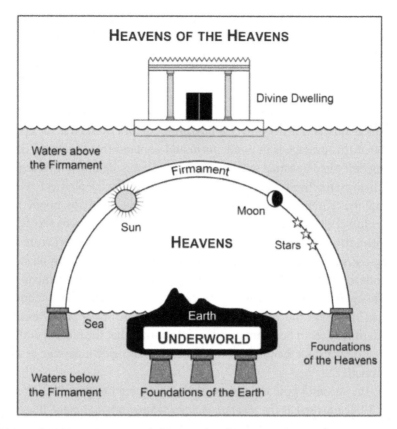

Fig 3-2. **The 3-Tier Universe.** Drawn by Kenneth Kully.

> Your attitude should be the same as that of Christ Jesus: Who, being
> in very nature God, did not consider equality with God something
> to be grasped, but made Himself nothing, taking the very nature
> of a servant, being made in human likeness. And being found in
> appearance as a man, He humbled Himself and became obedient
> to death—even death on a cross! Therefore God exalted him to the
> highest place and gave him the name that is above every name,
> that at the name of Jesus every knee should bow, *in heaven* and
> *on earth* and *under the earth*, and every tongue confess that Jesus
> Christ is Lord, to the glory of God the Father.
>
> Philippians 2:5–11 (my italics)

Ancient peoples understood the universe to be made up of three actual
and *physical* levels: (1) the heavenly realm, (2) the earthly world, and (3)
the underworld. Fig 3-2 presents this conceptualization of the structure

of the cosmos, and it will be explained in detail in the next section of this chapter. Today, Christians rarely recognize the incidental ancient science in Phil 2, but they correctly focus on the central Messages of Faith—the mystery of the Incarnation and the lordship of Jesus over the entire creation.

Of course, many Christians are quick to offer two common arguments against this 3-tier universe interpretation of Phil 2. First, they point out that this passage is in poetic form and contend that the world is not being described in actual or concrete terms. That is, figurative expressions are being employed, and consequently do not depict physical reality. Certainly, caution is necessary when interpreting the many poetic passages in Scripture, but this is not to say that poetry never refers to actual realities in nature. For example, Ps 148:3 features a poetic structure and states, "Praise the Lord, sun and moon, praise Him, all you shining stars." No one today doubts the existence of the sun, moon, and stars, and no one in the ancient world questioned the reality of these astronomical bodies either. Therefore, the *poetic language argument* must be applied carefully. Modern readers of Scripture need to determine what the biblical authors believed regarding the physical world before writing off a passage as simply "poetic."*

The second popular response to the interpretation that Phil 2 refers to a 3-tier universe is the *phenomenological language argument*. It asserts that Paul is describing the cosmos from his viewpoint, or phenomenological perspective. That is, the world "looks" or "appears" to have three tiers. So, in the same way that we now speak of the "rising" or "setting" of the sun, the apostle is using phenomenological language. According to this line of reasoning, Phil 2 does not affirm the reality of a world with three tiers. But there is a serious and subtle error in this argument. Did Paul use phenomenological language in the way that we do today? Would he agree with us if we told him that the so-called "rising" and "setting" of the sun are only visual effects caused by the rotation of our spherical planet? History reveals that Paul would disagree. The notion that the earth rotates

---

* It must also be pointed out that real historical people and events can appear in poetic passages. For example, the psalms are set in poetic frameworks and refer to Israel (65 times), David (14), and Moses (7). Christians do not dismiss these references as merely "poetic" and not corresponding to historical reality. Similarly, the writing off of Phil 2 because it appears in a poetic structure renders the kenosis of Jesus vulnerable to rejection. I doubt any Christian would want to do that.

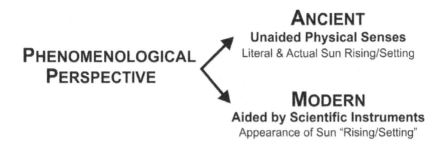

Fig 3-3. Categories of Phenomenological Perspective

daily on its axis causing the phenomenon of the sun to "rise" and "set" became accepted only in the 1600s after the work of Galileo.

Scripture does indeed employ phenomenological language to describe the natural world. But there is a critical and subtle difference between what the biblical writers saw and believed to be real in the universe, and what we today see and know to be a scientific fact. Observation in the ancient world was limited to unaided human senses, like the naked eye. But today scientific instruments, like telescopes, have broadened our view of the universe. As a result, it is essential to understand that statements in Scripture about nature are from an *ancient phenomenological perspective*. What the biblical writers and other ancient peoples saw with their eyes, they believed to be real, like the literal rising and setting of the sun. In contrast, we view the world from a *modern phenomenological perspective*. When we see the sun "rising" and "setting," we know that it is only an appearance or visual effect caused by the rotation of the earth. Therefore, it is crucial that these different viewpoints of nature not be confused and conflated. This is the problem with the popular phenomenological language argument—it reads the ancient science in Scripture through a modern perspective and mindset. Fig 3-3 distinguishes between ancient and modern phenomenological perspectives.

The Kenotic Hymn in Phil 2 can now be seen in a new light. When Paul wrote this passage he understood the structure of the universe from an ancient phenomenological perspective. Like most people at that time, unaided human senses led him to believe that the cosmos was literally made up of three actual and physical tiers. In other words, this apostle, under the inspiration of the Holy Spirit, employed the incidental science of his generation in order to declare the inerrant Messages of Faith that God took on human flesh in the person of Jesus to become a servant, and that the Father made Him Lord over the entire creation. Similar to Jesus' use of the mustard seed, Paul's intention in this passage is not to inform Christians of the structure of the physical world. It just happens to be that at the time he wrote this letter to the Philippian church, the 3-tier universe was his understanding of nature, and that of his readers. And like the central mystery revealed in the Kenotic Hymn, the Holy Spirit descended and humbled Himself by using ancient human ideas about nature in the revelatory process. Thus, ancient science is a vessel that helps to deliver Divine Theology in Scripture.

The challenge twenty-first century Christians face in reading the Bible is demonstrated by the way most people envision the shape of the earth in Gen 1:1–2. We are immersed in a scientific culture, surrounded by images of a spherical planet. The moment we see the word "earth" in this verse, a picture of a globe suspended in outer space immediately comes to mind, because we instinctively filter information through our intellectual categories. More precisely, we unconsciously read our modern science *into* the Bible. This interpretive error is termed eisegesis (Greek *eis*: in, into; *ēgeomai*: to guide). But everyone agrees that the goal of reading any text is to practice exegesis (*ek*: out, out of) and to draw *out* the author's intended meaning. Therefore, in order to understand biblical statements dealing with nature correctly, we need to suspend our scientific categories and attempt to think about the physical world like an ancient person thousands of years ago. In other words, we need to read Scripture through ancient eyes. No doubt about it, this is a very counterintuitive way to read.

THE 3-TIER UNIVERSE

In order to become comfortable with this counterintuitive reading approach to Scripture, I have found it helpful to focus on biblical passages that refer to the structure and operation of the earth and heavens. Today everyone knows that we live on a spherical planet that rotates on its axis and revolves around the sun. However, a careful examination of God's Word reveals that the inspired writers accepted a stationary universe with three tiers—the heavens above, the earth in between, and the underworld below (Fig 3-2). More specifically, the Bible views the physical world from an ancient phenomenological perspective, featuring an ancient geology and an ancient astronomy.

This section outlines nine basic characteristics of the 3-tier universe found in Scripture. Each section underlines the very logical process behind the conceptualization of the ancient science. We would have held the very same views about the natural world had we lived at that time. The biblical passages that are presented are also interpreted in light of the Message-Incident Principle. It will become obvious that ancient science plays an essential role in transporting the inerrant Word of God.

The Immobility of the Earth

Ancient geology assumed that the earth did not move. This is a reasonable idea from an ancient phenomenological perspective. Does anyone today sense that we are rotating on the earth's axis at 1,000 miles per hour and traveling around the sun at 65,000 mph? This phenomenon of immobility is so powerful that belief in a stationary earth was widely upheld until the 1600s. In fact, hard scientific evidence that the earth moved was only discovered in the 1800s with the construction of telescopes that could detect our movement through space.

The Old Testament clearly presents the immovability of the earth. Three verses repeat word-for-word, "The world is firmly established; it cannot move" (1 Chr 16:30; Pss 93:1, 96:10). Over twenty-five times, biblical writers use engineering terms like foundations and pillars to conceptualize the earth's stability. For example, Ps 104:5 states that, "God set the earth on its foundations; it can never be moved" (cf. 1 Sam 2:8; Ps 75:3; Job 38:4–6). The ancient Hebrews saw that mountains, hills, and plains remained constant throughout their lifetime, and they logically reasoned within their ancient intellectual category set that the earth was stationary. But more importantly, these passages reveal a Message of Faith. This incidental ancient geology delivers the inerrant revelation that God is the Creator and Sustainer of the world.

The Circumferential Sea and the Circular Earth

Ancient Near Eastern peoples thought that the earth was a circular island surrounded by a circumferential sea. Two phenomenological factors led to this idea. First, the constant visual impact of the horizon gives the impression that the world is enclosed within a circular boundary. Second, it was common knowledge at this time that journeys in any direction eventually led to a body of water. An appreciation of the geography in the region makes such a conclusion reasonable: the Mediterranean Sea is west, the Black and Caspian Seas are north, the Persian Gulf is east, and the

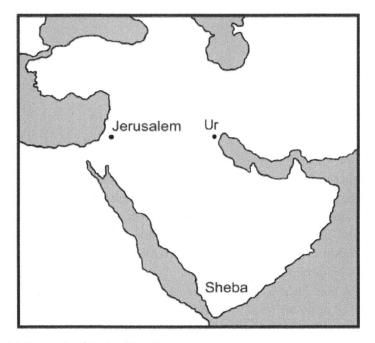

Fig 3-4. Geography of Ancient Near East

Arabian and Red Seas are south (Fig 3-4). A sixth-century BC Babylonian map of the world confirms the ancient notion of a sea encompassing a circular earth (Fig 3-5).

The circumferential sea is implied in Scripture. Proverbs 8:22–31 and Job 26:7–14 describe the creation of the world. The former states, "God inscribed a circle on the face of the deep" (v. 27); and the latter, "God has inscribed a circle on the surface of the waters" (v. 10). The Hebrew word translated as circle (*ḥûg*) refers to a two-dimensional geometric figure. It is sometimes rendered in English Bibles as horizon or compass, indicating a flat surface. Undoubtedly, Prov 8:27 and Job 26:10 depict the opening scene in the Bible when "darkness was over the surface of the deep, and the Spirit of God was hovering over the waters" (Gen 1:2). Therefore, instead of beginning with a sphere of water enveloping a global earth, as eisegetically pictured by most twenty-first century readers, God starts with a flat surface of water upon which He draws a circle to create the horizon.

In a verse that is well known to Christians, the Bible asserts that the earth is circular. The prophet Isaiah writes, "God sits enthroned above the circle of the earth, and its people are like grasshoppers. He stretches out

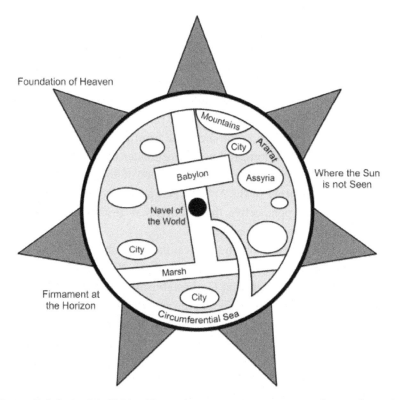

Fig 3-5. Babylonian World Map. This sixth-century BC map presents a flat circular earth bordered by a circumferential sea. The solid dome of heaven (firmament) comes to an end at the horizon and is supported by seven foundations/pillars. Redrawn by Kenneth Kully.

the heavens like a canopy, and spreads them out like a tent to live in" (Isa 40:22). Again, the Hebrew word translated as circle refers to a two-dimensional flat surface. The context of the verse complements this interpretation. Isaiah compares the universe to a tent that features a domed canopy over a flat floor. Psalms 19:4 and 104:2 also use the tent analogy to describe the structure of the world. Therefore, the correct understanding of Isa 40:22 is that God looks down from heaven and sees the entire earth and its circular border meeting the circumferential sea.

These two ancient geological notions led ancient Near Eastern peoples to believe that the earth literally came to an end at the shore of the great encompassing sea. This ancient science is reflected in Scripture nearly 50 times by the phrase "the ends of the earth." For example, God called Abraham from Ur, a city that was near the Persian Gulf (Gen 11:31; Heb 11:8). The Lord states, "O Israel My servant, Jacob, whom I have chosen, you descendants of Abraham My friend, I took you from the ends of the earth, and called you from its remotest parts" (Isa 41:8–9). Of course, the furthest land from Israel on a spherical earth is South America. But if the world was envisioned as an island, then understanding Ur to be at its edge was logical for those living in the ancient Near East. Similarly, in denouncing the "wicked and adulterous generation" of His day, Jesus proclaims, "The Queen of the South will rise at the judgment with this generation and condemn it; for she came from the ends of the earth to listen to Solomon's wisdom, and now One greater than Solomon is here" (Matt 12:42). The Lord is referring to the Queen of Sheba, whose land was in the southwest corner of the Arabian Peninsula. From an ancient Near Eastern geological perspective, this country was at end of the earth. Fig 3-4 identifies the sites of Ur and Sheba.

Clearly, the purpose of the biblical passages above is not to reveal the structure of the sea and the earth. Proverbs 8:27 and Job 26:10 deliver the Message of Faith that God established the boundaries of the creation. Similarly, Isa 40:22 reveals the spiritual truth that the Creator made the entire universe and that He sees the activities of every person. For Israel, Isa 41:8–9 was a comforting message that the Lord had personally chosen her to be His people. And to the corrupt generation in Jesus' day, Matt 12:24 was a warning that there will be a final judgment. But at the same time, "One greater than Solomon," the Son of God Himself, had descended to earth to reveal spiritual truths so that we can live our life with joy and fullness.

The Underside of the Earth and the Underworld

Ancient geology accepted that the earth had an underside and an underworld. Such notions are reasonable; we all experience the phenomena of places that are above and below us. The Old Testament refers to the underworld as *sh⁽e⁾ōl*, and English translations render this Hebrew word as grave, pit, and hell. In 40 of the 65 times that it appears, the context and associated terminology (e.g., going down to, depths of) indicates that *sh⁽e⁾ōl* is below the surface of the earth (Num 16:31–33; Prov 5:5; Isa 14:15). Similarly, the New Testament calls this region *hādes* and it is often translated as hell. In half of the 10 times this Greek word appears, the context presupposes a place below the earth's surface (Matt 11:23; Luke 10:15; Rev 20:14).

The New Testament also refers to a region "under the earth." The apostle John praises, "I heard every creature in heaven and on earth and under the earth and on the sea, and all that is in them, singing, 'To Him who sits on the throne and to the Lamb be praise and honor and power for ever and ever!'" (Rev 5:13; cf., Rev 5:3; Eph 4:9–10). As noted previously in the Kenotic Hymn, Paul writes that "at the name of Jesus every knee should bow, in heaven and on earth and under the earth" (Phil 2:10). Regrettably, English Bibles do not translate fully the original Greek. "Under the earth" should be rendered "the underworld." In fact, the Greek word *katachthoniōn* in this verse refers to the beings down (*kata*) in the chthonic (*chthovios*) or subterranean world. A more accurate translation of this verse is: At the name of Jesus every knee should bow—of beings in heaven, of beings on earth, and of beings in the underworld (cf., Matt 12:40; Eph 4:9–10; 1 Pet 3:19). For the biblical writers, the underworld and the underside of the earth were every bit as real as the heaven, earth, and sea. These terms are not poetic figures of speech, nor are they only an "appearance" or merely "phenomenological" as some understand them today.

When we apply the Message-Incident Principle to Phil 2:10 and Rev 5:13, it becomes evident that the purpose of these verses is not to reveal that the universe has three physical tiers. Rather, the Holy Spirit employs ancient scientific concepts that refer to the totality and immensity of the cosmos. The divine revelation in these verses is that Jesus is Lord over every region of the entire creation.

The Flat Earth

The Bible never specifically states that the earth is flat. Rather, scriptural evidence from the terms and contexts of passages indicates that this ancient geological notion was assumed to be a fact by the inspired writers and their readers. In the same way that we see the word earth and automatically visualize a spherical planet, they immediately pictured a flat surface. In light of the ancient geological features presented above, the biblical authors believed that the earth was like a round coffee table with edges, an underside shelf, and stable legs.

The idea that the earth was flat is perfectly logical from an ancient phenomenological perspective. Anyone looking out from an elevated position perceives the world to be a level plain bordered by the horizon. This ancient geology is reflected in the temptation of Jesus. Matthew 4:8 states,

"Again the devil took Jesus to a very high mountain and showed Him all the kingdoms of the world and their splendor." The Greek word translated into English as "world" is *kosmos*, which literally means the entire universe or sum total of everything that exists. But everyone knows that there were great civilizations in China and the Americas at this time, and no matter how tall this mountain might have been, it was not possible for Jesus to see *all* the kingdoms of the world.

Separating the Message of Faith from the incidental ancient science in Matt 4:8 avoids a needless conflict or contradiction between the Bible and modern geology. The Holy Spirit's intention was not to reveal earth science in this verse. Rather, God used the geology-of-the-day as a vessel to deliver the inerrant revelation that in taking on our very humanity, Jesus was tempted by the devil in every way that we are. But instead of falling into sin, our Lord and Savior was victorious!

The Daily Movement of the Sun across the Sky

Ancient astronomy assumed that the sun literally crossed the sky each day. Experiencing the phenomenon of the sun traveling from east to west led the biblical writers without hesitation to incorporate this idea into Scripture. As the psalmist proclaims, "The sun rises at one end of the heavens and makes its circuit to the other" (Ps 19:6). Similarly, King Solomon writes, "The sun rises and the sun sets, and hurries back to where it rises" (Eccl 1:5; cf., Ps 50:1). And Jesus accommodated to His listeners by saying that our Father in heaven "causes His sun to rise on evil and good" (Matt 5:45). In total, the Bible makes over 60 references to the sun's daily movement across the sky.

Of course, no one today accepts that the sun actually rises and sets. Though it certainly looks like it does, our *modern phenomenological perspective* recognizes that this is only an appearance, when in actual fact the earth is rotating on its axis to produce this visual effect. Similarly, our use of the phrases "the setting sun" and "the rising sun" are now poetic and figurative expressions that are informed by modern astronomy. But as noted earlier, in ancient times the physical world was understood through an *ancient phenomenological perspective*. What ancient peoples saw with their eyes, they believed to be literally true. For them, the sun actually moved across the sky and the phrases "the setting sun" and "the rising sun" were concrete facts of nature. In order to deal with this conflict between Scripture and science, the Message-Incident Principle assists us in separating this ancient astronomy from the Divine Theology. The purpose of passages that refer to the movement of the sun is to reveal God's creatorship and lordship over the sun, not its position and operation in the heavens.

The Firmament

Ancient astronomers believed that the circular earth and circumferential sea were enclosed by a firm dome overhead. From an ancient phenomenological point of view, the vault of the sky certainly appears to be a solid immovable structure, similar to an inverted bowl. Early English translations of the Bible, like the King James Version, refer to it as "the firmament." For example, on the second day of creation God said, " 'Let there be a firmament in the midst of the waters, and let it divide the waters from the waters.' And God made the firmament, and divided the waters which were under the firmament from the waters which were above the firmament: and it was so. And God called the firmament 'Heaven'" (Gen 1:6–8). Similarly, the KJV renders Ps 19:1 as "The heavens declare the glory of God and the firmament sheweth His handywork."

Everyone knows that there is no solid structure above the earth. Some modern translations of the Bible attempt to resolve this conflict between Scripture and science by using the word "expanse" instead of firmament.[3] In doing so, they give the impression that on the second creation day God creates a vast empty region, alluding to outer space and the earth's atmosphere. However, this betrays the meaning of the Hebrew word *rāqîaʿ*. The root of this noun is the verb *rāqaʿ* which means to flatten, stamp down, spread out, and hammer out. That is, this Hebrew verb carries a sense of flattening something solid rather than opening a broad empty space. Exodus 39:3 and Isa 40:19 use *rāqaʿ* for pounding metals into thin plates, and Num 16:38 employs the related word *riqqûaʿ* (broad plate) in a similar context. The verb *rāqaʿ* is even found in a passage referring to the creation of the sky, which is understood to be a firm surface like a metal. Job 37:18 asks, "Can you join God in spreading out the skies, hard as a mirror of cast bronze?" (cf., Exod 24:10; Job 22:14; Ezek 1:22).

Early translations of Scripture conserve the original sense of *rāqîaʿ*. The Greek Old Testament, called the Septuagint and dated about 250 BC, renders this Hebrew word as *stereōma*, which means the vault of heaven. This noun is related to the adjective *stereos*, a common term for firm, hard, and solid. The importance of the Septuagint cannot be overstated, since New Testament writers often used it in quoting Old Testament passages. Similarly, the Latin translation of the Bible, known as the Vulgate, translates *rāqîa'* as *firmamentum*. This word is related to the adjective *firmus*, from which derives the English word firm. The Latin Bible was written during the fifth century AD and served the Church for over one thousand years. Its impact upon early English translations, like the King James Version, is clear in that they render *rāqîa'* as firmament. Thus, the *traditional* and *conservative* understanding of this Hebrew term, as reflected in the early translations of the Bible, is that God created a solid structure over the earth on the second day of creation.

Being aware of the meaning of the term firmament sheds light on biblical passages that refer to "the foundations/pillars of the heavens" (Job 26:11; 2 Sam 22:8) and "the ends of the heavens" (Deut 4:32; Isa 13:5; Ps 19:6; Matt 24:31). These are reasonable notions from an ancient phenomenological view point. In the eyes of ancient peoples, the firmament did not move. Thus, it must have been placed on something solid and immovable, like the pillars or foundations set down by ancient builders. The visual impact of the horizon also led to the logical conclusion that the dome of heaven had ends (see Fig 3-2). However, the purpose of Scripture is not to reveal the actual structure of the heavens. Rather, by stating that "the firmament proclaims the work of God's hands" in Ps 19, the Holy Spirit employs an ancient astronomical notion as a vessel to reveal the inerrant theological truth that the heavens reflect intelligent design and point to the Creator.

The Waters Above in the Heavens

Ancient Near Eastern astronomy assumed that the firmament supported a body of water over the earth. As unusual as this notion seems to our twenty-first century scientific mindset, such a conclusion is very logical from an ancient phenomenological perspective. The color of the sky's dome is a changing blue, similar to a lake or sea. As well, rain falls to the ground from above. These ancient peoples had no way of knowing that the blue of the heavens was a visual effect due to the scattering of short wave light in the upper atmosphere.

The Bible affirms the existence of a heavenly sea. As noted previously, Gen 1:6–8 states that the Creator made a firmament to separate the "waters above" from the "waters below" (the latter being the earthly sea, as named in Gen 1:10). In Ps 104:2–3, "God stretches out the heavens like a tent and lays the beams of His upper chambers on their waters" (cf., Ezek 28:2). Calling forth praise from the sun, moon, and stars, Ps 148:4 appeals to this heavenly sea, "Praise the Lord you highest heavens and you waters above the skies." And Jer 10:12–13 records, "God stretches out the heavens by His understanding. When He thunders, the waters in the heavens roar." Some Christians attempt to argue that the water mentioned in these passages is water vapor. However, biblical Hebrew has three well-known words (*ʾēd, nāśîʾ, ʿānān*) that refer to mist, vapor, or cloud (Gen 2:6; Jer 10:13; Gen 9:13, respectively), and the inspired writers did not use them in these passages.

The waters above do not correspond to any physical reality known to modern astronomy. This fact directly challenges scientific concordism. But this problem vanishes in light of the Message-Incident Principle. The Holy Spirit accommodated to the ancient astronomy of the Hebrews in order to reveal that God created the visually dominant blue "structure" overhead. And this inerrant divine disclosure remains steadfast for us—the Creator made the phenomenon of the blue sky.

The Sun, Moon, and Stars in the Firmament

Ancient peoples believed that the sun, moon, and stars were set in the firmament. This is another reasonable idea. These astronomical bodies appear to be in front of a blue heavenly sea and positioned in the surface of a structure holding it up. The Bible affirms this ancient astronomy. On the fourth day of creation, God said:

> "Let there be lights in the firmament of heaven to separate the day from the night, and let them serve as signs to mark seasons and days and years, and let them be lights in the firmament of heaven to give light on the earth." And it was so. God made two great lights—the greater light to govern the day and the lesser light to govern the night. He also made the stars. God set them in the firmament of heaven to give light on the earth, to govern the day and the night, and to separate light from darkness. And God saw it was good. And there was evening, and there was morning—the fourth day.
>
> Genesis 1:14–19

Some Christians attempt to harmonize this passage with modern astronomy. They suggest that the Hebrew word traditionally translated as firmament refers to the expanse of outer space. But as noted previously, this is not the meaning of *rāqîaʿ*.

The purpose of the fourth creation day is to reveal a radical theological message to the ancient world. It is a polemic (a cutting critique) against pagan astral religion. Most people at that time believed that the sun, moon, and stars were gods. But the biblical author, through the Holy Spirit, strips these astronomical bodies of their divine status and makes them mere creations of the Hebrew God. Even more radically, the Scripture throws these so-called "gods" into servitude! Instead of men and women serving the heavenly bodies as demanded by astrological religions, the inspired writer states that the sun, moon, and stars were created to serve humanity. In other words, the Bible puts the heavenly bodies in their proper place. They have value because they are God's good creations, but they are definitely not gods worthy of worship.

Ancient astronomy also assumed that stars are quite small and that they sometimes dislodged from the firmament and fell to the earth. Undoubtedly, their appearance as luminous specks against the night sky, as well as the sighting of a streaking meteor, led to this very rational idea. And it appears in Scripture. Stars both fall to the earth (Isa 34:4; Matt 24:29; Rev 6:13) and can be thrown down to it (Dan 8:10; Rev 12:4). The Bible employs this ancient astronomy to describe the disassembling of the heavens at the end of the world on judgment day. God will shake the firmament, causing the stars to fall to earth, and then He will roll up this heavenly structure. Isaiah envisions the end time in this way: "All the stars of the heavens will be dissolved and the sky rolled up like a scroll; all the starry host will fall like withered leaves from the vine, like shrivelled figs from the fig tree" (Isa 34:4). Similarly, Jesus prophesies that at "the coming of the Son of Man . . . the stars will fall from the sky, and the heavenly bodies will be shaken" (Matt 24:27, 29).

All these Scriptures make perfect sense from an ancient phenomenological point of view. Stars were small enough to fall to the earth, and the firmament, which was depicted as a tent canopy being spread out at the beginning of the world, would be rolled up at the end of time. To be sure, caution is required when interpreting end times passages because they feature poetic language. But this is not to say that everything mentioned in prophecies has no correspondence to the real world, and consequently can be written off as merely figurative. For example, Isa 34 and Matt 24 refer to astronomical realities: heaven, earth, stars, and other heavenly bodies. No one denies their existence. In the same way that the biblical writers literally believed in the ancient astronomy describing the assembly of the heavens, they also accepted the literal disassembly of these structures at the final judgment. The Message of Faith in these passages is not a revelation about the structure of the heavens. Instead, their purpose is to reveal that the world will come to an end and there will be a day of judgment when each of us will have to give an account for our life. And you can count on it happening.

The Lower Heavens and the Upper Heavens

Ancient Near Eastern peoples believed that the heavens were made up of two basic regions—the lower heavens and the upper heavens. The former includes the atmosphere, the firmament with its luminary bodies, and the sea of waters above. The latter is the celestial realm where God/s and other celestial beings reside. It is important to emphasize that according to these ancients, both regions are real *physical* locations, with the upper heavens resting upon the lower heavens. The Bible features this ancient astronomy.

The Hebrew word for heavens is *shāmayim*. It carries many meanings and the context of the passage in which it appears usually determines its interpretation. This term can refer to the dome of heaven as seen on the second day of creation when "God called the firmament 'heavens' " (Gen 1:7). It can also mean air or atmosphere as found in the phrases "the birds of the heavens" (Gen 2:19–20) and "the clouds of heaven" (Dan 7:13). *Shāmayim* includes the waters above the firmament. As the psalmist writes, "God stretches out the heavens like a tent and lays the beams of His upper chambers on their waters" (Ps 104:2–3; cf., Ps 148:4). This verse also identifies the location of the Creator's celestial dwelling place. It rests upon the heavenly sea. From an ancient perspective, the prayers of the Hebrews make sense. "Look down from heaven, Your holy dwelling place, and bless Your people Israel" (Deut 26:15; cf., Ps 33:13–14; Isa 40:22). Occasionally in the Old Testament, the upper heavens are called *shāmayim shāmayim* (literally, heavens of heavens) and are translated "highest heavens." For example, "God made the heavens, the highest heavens with all their host, and the earth and all that is on it" (Neh 9:6; cf., 1 Kgs 8:27; Ps 148:4).

In the New Testament, the distinct heavenly structures of ancient astronomy are collapsed into one Greek word, making it difficult at times to understand and translate. *Ouranos* is rendered in English Bibles as heaven and sky. In the lower heavens, this term refers to the atmosphere or air as seen in the phrases "the birds of the heaven" (Matt 6:26; Luke

9:58) and "the clouds of heaven" (Matt 26:64; Mark 14:62). *Ouranos* can also mean the firmament since it is opened (John 1:51; Acts 7:56), shaken (Matt 24:29; Heb 12:26), and rolled up (Heb 1:12; Rev 6:14). The waters above are implied since the sky can be shut from rainfall (Luke 4:25; Rev 11:6). Regarding the upper heavens, *ouranos* refers to where God and His angels dwell in many New Testament passages (Luke 22:43; Mark 12:25; John 6:38). For example, "As Jesus was coming up out of the water, He saw heaven being torn open and the Spirit descending on Him like a dove. And a voice came from heaven: 'You are my Son, whom I love; with You I am well pleased'" (Mark 1:10–11).

To summarize, the Bible definitely presents a 3-tier universe as illustrated in Fig 3-2 on page 47. This view of the cosmos was the best science-of-the-day thousands of years ago in the ancient Near East, and it was accepted by the inspired writers of God's Word and their readers.[4] References in Scripture to the earth set on immovable foundations, the heavens being similar to a tent canopy, and the rising and setting sun are not fanciful poetic statements. These verses were intended to describe the literal structure and actual operation of the world. The use of common objects, like tents and building foundations, were analogies meant to convey the genuine arrangement of the heavens and the earth. However, it is clear that the biblical understanding of geology and astronomy does not correspond to physical reality. Scientific concordism fails.

Even though this is the case, it is necessary to emphasize that the incidental ancient geology and astronomy play an essential role in Scripture. They are vessels that deliver inerrant Messages of Faith, and they do so with proficiency. Evidence for this comes from Christians in every generation, because in reading Scripture, they have understood the foundational spiritual truth that the God of the Bible is the sovereign Creator and Sustainer of the heavens and earth. Of course, recognizing the ancient science in Scripture is at first challenging, especially for a modern generation like ours. And reading beyond this ancient phenomenological perspective of nature is quite counterintuitive. Yet with time and practice this is possible, and it is particularly important in the origins debate.

An implication regarding the ancient view of the world's structure and operation in Scripture is that the Bible should also have an ancient understanding of origins. And since the geology and astronomy in the Word of God are ancient, consistency argues that there should be an ancient biology. Stated precisely, the biblical origins accounts might feature an ancient phenomenological perspective on the origin of life and death, including the beginning of human life and death. But before we look at these intriguing notions, a few well-known concordist interpretations can now be reconsidered.

Excursus: Scientific Concordism in Isaiah 40 and Job 26?

Two popular verses that Christians often use to "prove" that modern science appears in the Bible are Isa 40:22 and Job 26:7.[5] The former is presented simply as, "God sits enthroned above the circle of the earth;" and the latter, "God spreads out the northern skies over empty space, and suspends the earth over nothing." Read through a twenty-first century scientific mindset, Isa 40 could be seen as depicting the outline of planet earth from outer space, and Job 26 as referring to it being suspended by gravitational forces. If these are correct interpretations, then modern science was placed in Scripture well before scientists discovered these facts of nature. Scientific concordists argue that only a God who transcends time could have revealed such information ahead of time, and consequently, this is solid evidence that the Bible is divinely inspired.

However, these two examples are classic *biblical proof texts.* They are ripped out of context and then manipulated by reading into them (eisegesis) notions that were never intended by the human author or the Holy Spirit. As noted earlier, Isa 40:22 in its entirety reads, "God sits enthroned above the circle of the earth, and its people are like grasshoppers. He stretches out the heavens like a canopy, and spreads them out like a tent to live in." Clearly, this verse reflects a 3-tiered universe. The cosmos is compared to a tent, with a domed canopy above and a flat floor below. This is an analogy that is used in Scripture to describe the structure of the world (Pss 19:4–5, 104:2–3). Moreover, the ancient science in Isa 40:22 is consistent with other passages in this biblical book. Isaiah asserts that at the judgment "the sky will be rolled up like a scroll" and "all the starry host will fall" to earth (34:4). He also claims that God is "the Creator of the ends of the earth" (40:28) and that He took Abraham "from the ends of the earth, from its remotest parts" (41:9). Thus, Isa 40:22 must be interpreted in its context and in light of ancient science. The circle of the earth refers to the circumferential shore of a flat circular earth (Fig 3-5; p. 53).

The scientific concordist interpretation of Job 26:7 also tears this verse out of the context of its chapter and book. Ancient astronomy is clearly seen a few verses later with "The pillars of the heavens quake, aghast at God's rebuke" (26:11). Belief that the heavens had foundations makes sense because the inspired author accepted the reality of the firmament, as seen in the question, "Can you join God in spreading out the skies, hard as a mirror of cast bronze?" (37:18). The location of the divine dwelling in the 3-tier universe is reflected in another question, "Who can understand how He thunders from His pavilion?" (36:29). In other words, the Lord lives just overhead in a place where the rumble of thunder arises. The book of Job also features ancient geology. "God unleashes His lightning beneath the whole heaven and sends it to the ends of the earth" (37:3), "He shakes the earth from its place and makes its pillars tremble" (9:6), and He asks, "Where were you when I laid the earth's foundation?" (38:4). In addition, the Hebrew word *tālāh*, which is translated as "suspends" in Job 26:7, appears in the context of hanging up an object, like a utensil on a peg (Isa 22:24), weapons on a wall (Ezek 27:10), or a lyre on a tree (Ps 137:2). Job 26:7 does not refer to hovering in empty space; it simply states that the earth is not hung from anything in the universe.

The scientific concordist interpretations of Isa 40:22 and Job 26:7 are proof texts. Regrettably, many Christians rip these verses out of Scripture and their ancient scientific context, and then conflate them with modern scientific ideas. The popular concordist understandings of the circle of the earth and the suspension of the earth over nothing are unbiblical.

INERRANCY, ACCOMMODATION, AND BIBLICAL INSPIRATION

Conservative Christian theology is distinguished by the belief in biblical inerrancy. Commonly understood, this notion asserts that God inspired Scripture, and as a result, it is completely free from any errors. Of course, a high view of biblical inspiration is foundational to the best theology. However, most Christians conflate the concept of biblical inerrancy with a strict literal interpretation of Scripture. They often assume that statements in the Bible about the structure, operation, and origin of the world are completely factual and in alignment with physical reality. In other words, a majority of Christians are scientific concordists, and they believe that inerrancy extends to scientific statements in Scripture.

But as Fig 3-6 reveals, scientific concordism fails. We do not live in a 3-tier universe. The earth is not flat, circular, and stationary. The sun, moon, and stars are not embedded in a firmament that holds up a sea of water overhead. The ancient view of nature in God's Word challenges the

HEAVENS & EARTH IN SCRIPTURE

Structures	Reality
Flat circular earth with ends, foundations & underworld	No
Flat circumferential sea around earth & bordered by horizon	No
Firmament overhead in heaven & set on foundations	No
Sun, moon & stars set in firmament	No
Sea of waters above in heaven & held up by firmament	No
Beams of divine dwelling set in sea of waters above	No

Operations

Earth stationary & immovable	No
Sun moves daily across sky & under horizon	No
Sun, moon & stars move through firmament	No
Stars ocassionally fall to earth	No

Fig 3-6. The Failure of Scientific Concordism

common understanding of biblical inerrancy. Serious questions immediately arise the moment Christians recognize that statements about nature in the Bible do not correspond to physical reality: Why is there a conflict instead of an accord between Scripture and science? Did the Holy Spirit make a mistake in the revelatory process? Or asked more bluntly, does God lie in the Bible?

Principle of Biblical Accommodation

Let me answer the last question very directly: NO! God does NOT lie in the Bible. Lying requires deceptive and malicious intent, and the Lord is not a God of deception and maliciousness. In fact, Scripture itself states that God "does not lie" because "it is impossible for God to lie" (Titus 1:2; Heb 6:18). Instead, when the Holy Spirit inspired the writers of the Bible, He *accommodated.* He lowered Himself and met them and their readers at their level. In the same way that Jesus meets us wherever we happen to be, so too the Holy Spirit inspired the authors of Scripture by using their terms and concepts about the natural world in order to reveal as effectively as possible Messages of Faith. Some Christians might assume that accommodation waters down the Bible. Not true. Four basic arguments support the principle of biblical accommodation:

- Divine accommodation is a consequence of divine revelation. That is, built into the notion that God reveals to humans is the fact that the Infinite Creator has to descend to the level of finite creatures in order to communicate.

- The principle of accommodation is a critical aspect of the ultimate act of divine revelation—the Incarnation. According to Phil 2:7–8, God "humbled Himself" and "made Himself nothing" in order to become a man in the person of Jesus and to reveal His unfathomable love for us.

- Jesus accommodated in His teaching ministry. He often employed parables. These are earthly stories that deliver heavenly messages. At times, the Lord included ancient scientific notions, like the mustard seed being the smallest of all seeds, to communicate a divine revelation to His listeners.

- Finally, accommodation is experienced and even used by Christians today. In prayer, does the Lord not descend and speak to us through our intellectual categories? And when a four-year-old asks "the question" about where babies come from, parents answer by coming down to the level of the child. They communicate the central message—a baby is a gift from God when a mom and dad love each other—without presenting the incidental details of sex.

The principle of accommodation also shapes modern translations of the Bible. It is most prominent in Eugene Peterson's *The Message*, which attempts to present the Scripture's "ideas in everyday language."[6] For example, he translates the mustard seed parable in Matt 13:31–32 as: "God's kingdom is like a pine nut that a farmer plants. It is quite small as seeds go, but in the course of years it grows into a huge pine tree, and eagles build nests in it." Peterson definitely delivers the Message of Faith that Jesus intended, but substitutes the ancient botany regarding the mustard seed with that of a tree known to people in America today. In this translation the power of the inerrant Word of God transcends the incidental use of a pine nut.

Keeping all of this in mind, we can accommodate the biblical accounts of origins to our generation. For example, Gen 1:1–5 could be rewritten with modern scientific concepts:

> [1]During billions of years God created the heavens and the earth through evolution.
>
> [2]Now the world did not exist before the creation of space, time, and matter.

³And God said, "Let there be an explosion." And there was an explosion.

⁴God saw it was good, and He separated the explosion from nothingness.

⁵God called the explosion "The Big Bang." This was the first cosmological epoch.

Again, the eternal Messages of Faith are preserved—the foundational beliefs that God created the world and that the creation is good. This Divine Theology is delivered employing an incidental modern science that is familiar to many of us today. And should a better scientific theory than evolution be discovered in the future, the inerrant messages of Gen 1:1–5 will be easily re-accommodated to this new understanding of origins.

Toward an Incarnational Approach to Biblical Inerrancy

The greatest act of divine revelation is the Incarnation (Latin *in*: in; *carnis*: flesh). God taking on human flesh in the person of Jesus provides us with parallels to help appreciate biblical inerrancy and to understand how the Holy Spirit inspired the biblical writers in passages that refer to the physical world.[7] Instructive similarities appear between Scripture and: (1) the dual nature of the Lord, (2) His entering the world at a certain point in history, and (3) His teaching style in proclaiming the Good News.

A central Christian belief is that the Lord is both fully divine and fully human. As a man, Jesus undoubtedly experienced the limits and problems of a physical body—the need for food and sleep, common aches and pains, etc. Consequently, God's ultimate act of revelation came through a fallible and imperfect human vessel. Most Christians would also agree that whether the Lord was six feet tall or five foot two, His actual height was not essential to the gospel He proclaimed. In other words, Jesus' specific human characteristics are incidental to the Good News. Inerrancy rests in the Messages of Faith the Lord preached, and not in the less-than-perfect earthly vessel through which He delivered them.

Similar to Jesus, the Bible itself features both divine and human characteristics. For example, the New Testament is written in Koine Greek (*koine*: common). This ancient language is an unrefined form of Greek that was spoken by the average person in the streets. Today it is a dead language, because no community uses it. Yet despite these characteristics, Koine Greek still transports divinely inspired Messages of Faith. In fact, our primary source of knowledge about Jesus comes through this undignified language. Some Christians might assume that the Holy Spirit employed the most sophisticated form of Greek at that time, but this is not the case. Therefore, it is possible for an imperfect vessel, like a dead ancient street language, to transport God's inerrant Word.

Christian faith asserts that Jesus both transcends time and has entered into human history. In other words, God accommodated by leaving eternity to enter into the creaturely boundaries of time. As a consequence, the Lord's life and ministry were adapted to an ancient Palestinian period. He worked a typical job as a carpenter, ate the foods of the day, and taught parables using the common ideas of the people. Is it not conceivable, then, that the Incarnation could have occurred at another point in history, revealing the identical inerrant message of salvation? For example, if Jesus came to America today, He might be in a computer-related occupation, probably consume Coke and Big Macs, and would employ modern science in some parables. In other words, the actual point in history when Jesus came into the world is ultimately incidental.

Like Jesus' temporality, the Bible both transcends time and is bound within history. Scripture offers timeless truth written during various ancient historical periods. The actual points in history when the Holy Spirit inspired the sacred writers are incidental to the inerrant Messages of Faith. That is, there is nothing inherently special about any specific point in the past. In the same way that the Lord's timeless nature rises above His historicity, the eternal truths in Scripture transcend the ancient historical conditions during which they were revealed. Evidence for this fact is seen in the lives of men and women forever changed by the Gospel in every generation. The Message of Faith is not only relevant for people in the past, but also for us today, and for those in the future.

Jesus taught the Word of God using the words of humans. In order to deliver the Gospel as effectively as possible, He accommodated to the intellectual level of the men and women around Him. Notably, the Lord often used parables. These are stories in which the events that are mentioned never actually happened. This is powerful evidence that divine revelation is not limited to only literal and historical statements. Jesus also employed an imperfect ancient science, like the size of the mustard seed, to teach about the kingdom of God. But instructing in this way does not undermine the inerrancy of the spiritual messages. Rather, this technique makes the Gospel more accessible to an ancient audience. Undoubtedly, had Jesus lived today He would teach employing the marvelous discover-

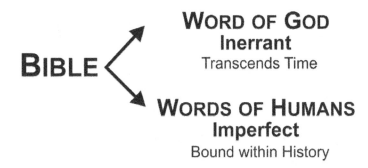

Fig 3-7. An Incarnational Approach to Biblical Inerrancy

ies of science. Thanks to the microscope, the mustard seed parable might be re-accommodated as: The kingdom of God is like a moss spore that falls to the ground; it is the smallest of all seeds, but when grown it is the widest of plants, extending across the forest floor, so that tiny creatures come and make their home in it.[8]

Similar to the teaching method employed by Jesus, the Bible is the Word of God delivered in the words of humans. The Lord's repeated use of parables opens the door to the possibility that the Holy Spirit revealed Messages of Faith in passages referring to events that never actually occurred in the past. Parts of Scripture, such as the accounts of origins in the book of Genesis, may feature non-literal and non-historical statements in order to facilitate the communication of Divine Theology. In addition, the presence of ancient science in Jesus' teachings indicates that an imperfect understanding of nature can deliver inerrant spiritual truths. His use of the science-of-the-day also offers a significant precedent: If evolution is true, then there is no reason why the biblical origins accounts could not be re-accommodated for our generation by using modern evolutionary science as an incidental vessel to transport the Messages of Faith in Gen 1–3. Chapter 6 will explore this intriguing possibility.

To conclude, Fig 3-7 depicts an approach to biblical inerrancy that reflects features of the Incarnation. The correspondence to the Message-Incident Principle is obvious. The Message of Faith is the inerrant and timeless Word of God, while incidental ancient science aligns with the imperfect and historically conditioned words of humans. The present chapter demonstrates that scientific concordism fails. Consequently, biblical inerrancy does not extend to statements about the structure and operation of the physical world. Yet, Scripture itself proves that an errant ancient science can reveal Holy Spirit-inspired eternal truths. In the illuminating light of Jesus, we can now see that *the Bible is the inerrant Word of God that transcends time, written in the imperfect words of humans bound within history.*[9]

4

The Biblical Accounts of Origins

THE FIRST THREE CHAPTERS of the Bible are foundational to Christian faith. They include well-known accounts of the origin of the world in six days, the creation of Adam and Eve in the garden of Eden, and their fall into sin. Today, over half of American adults believe that the events recorded in the biblical origins accounts are "literally true, meaning it happened that way word-for-word."[1] Nearly 90% of born-again Christians accept this literal interpretation. They claim that the Holy Spirit dictated to secretary-like biblical writers scientific facts about the creation of the world and the earliest activities of humans. For these believers, scientific concordism in Gen 1–3 is a fundamental component of their faith and origins position.

It has long been acknowledged that Scripture describes actual events from the past. The scientific discipline of biblical archaeology explores the history of ancient Palestine and the surrounding regions. Evidence collected from archaeological sites confirms the existence of many customs, places, and peoples referred to in the Bible. However, some born-again Christians reject scientific concordism. They do not believe that the events recorded in Gen 1–3 actually happened, and in particular, they do not accept the existence of Adam and Eve. This minority of believers, which includes evolutionary creationists, claims that actual history begins roughly around Gen 12 with God's calling of Abraham to the Promised Land.[2]

Conservative Christians who reject scientific concordism in Gen 1–3 are quick to point out that the Holy Spirit did not intend to offer an outline of God's actual creative events at the beginning of time. Instead, the Bible opens with Divine Theology. Scripture reveals that the Lord created the universe and life, the creation is very good, only humans are made in

MESSAGE
Divine Theology
God created the world
The world is very good
Humans created in Image of God
Humans are sinful
God judges humans for sin

INCIDENT
Ancient Science of Origins
Ancient Phenomenological
Perspective

Fig 4-1. Genesis 1–3 and the Message-Incident Principle

the Image of God, everyone has fallen into sin, and He judges us for our sinfulness. In reading Gen 1–3, these Christians use the Message-Incident Principle to interpret statements about the origin of the world and humanity. They believe that the first three chapters of Scripture feature an incidental *ancient science of origins* that delivers inerrant Messages of Faith about the creation and the human spiritual condition. Fig 4-1 introduces Gen 1–3 in light of the Message-Incident Principle.

This is certainly a very challenging approach to understanding the biblical accounts of origins. Personally, I found it threatening when I first heard of it, since I was a diehard scientific concordist and young earth creationist. In fact, I mocked Christians who held this viewpoint, including some of my former professors in seminary (and yes, I regret my bad behavior and have since apologized). But graduate school in theology introduced me to the biblical evidence, like that outlined in the previous chapter, and it slowly became clear that Scripture incorporates an ancient science of the structure and operation of the world. Logically it followed that the Word of God must also feature an ancient science of origins. Indeed, where the biblical facts eventually led me was quite a shock, to say the least.

This chapter presents evidence to challenge the popular belief that scientific concordism is a foundational component of Gen 1–3. No doubt about it, many Christians will find this troubling at first. Yet like in the last chapter, I will use an inductive Bible study method. The interpretive assumption previously embraced is recast: As the Word of God judges the thoughts of our heart and remodels our mind (Heb 4:12; Rom 12:1–2), so too features in Gen 1–3 must lead us to evaluate and reshape our view of how the Holy Spirit revealed Himself through the inspired writers in these opening chapters. Or to state it more incisively, if Scripture itself indicates that events like the creation of the world in six days never happened, then we must submit to this evidence in the Word of God.

GENESIS 1: THE CREATION WEEK

Throughout the ages, most Christians have believed that Gen 1 is a basic outline of God's actual creative acts in the origin of the universe and life. Understandably, the many references to time in this first chapter have led to the assumption that this is a historical account: the opening phrase (in the beginning), the orderly sequence of divine interventions over six days, the concluding sentence of each creation day (there was evening and there was morning), and the blessing of the seventh day as a day of rest. However, ancient poetic features and ancient scientific notions argue against scientific concordism in the first chapter of the Bible.

Fig 4-2 illustrates that Gen 1 is structured on a pair of parallel panels. Use of this ancient poetic framework is a response to the formless (Hebrew *tōhû*) and empty (*bōhû*) world described in Gen 1:2. These rhyming words would have caught the attention of the Hebrews. During the first three days of creation, God deals with the problem of formlessness by defining the boundaries of the universe. In the last three days, He fills the world with heavenly bodies and living creatures to resolve the emptiness. Parallels emerge between the two panels. On the first day of creation, God creates light in alignment with the fourth day's placement of the sun, moon, and stars in the firmament. The separation of the waters above from the waters below on the second creation day provides an air space for birds and a sea for marine creatures, both of which are made on the fifth day. And during the third creation day, God commands dry land to appear followed by plants and fruit-bearing trees in anticipation of the sixth day and the origin of land animals and humans, and their need for food.

Recognizing the parallel panels in Gen 1 resolves a well-known "contradiction" often presented by people who reject the Bible and Christianity. Skeptics argue that it is not possible for light to exist on the first day of creation, because the sun doesn't appear until the fourth day. But this so-called "conflict" instantly disappears if modern readers respect the ancient poetic framework in the opening chapter of Scripture. The

FORMLESS
tōhû

Day 1

Separate
Day
Night

Day 2

Separate
Waters Above
Waters Below

Day 3

Separate
Water
Land
(Plants)

EMPTY
bōhû

Day 4

Decorate
Sun
Moon & Stars

Day 5

Decorate
Flying Creatures
Sea Creatures

Day 6

Decorate
Land Animals
Humans
(Plants for Food)

Day 7
Sabbath

Fig 4-2. Genesis 1 Parallel Panels

presence of parallel panels in Gen 1 is clear evidence of poetic license (or freedom) and indicates that this account is not a strict literal record. In other words, the biblical author never intended to offer a list of the divine acts of creation in a chronological sequence.

The Holy Spirit-inspired writer also structured Gen 1 around the Sabbath Commandment. By placing God's creative work in the first six days and His rest on the seventh day, he achieves a theological purpose. This poetic framework is a model or typology affirming the Fourth Commandment. As everyone knows, actual events in the past do not unfold in such a patterned and artificial fashion. Historical records of the inanimate world and living organisms have never corresponded to the Hebrew work week and Sabbath, or to parallel panels. Consequently, the young creationist argument that appeals to Exod 20:11—For in six days the Lord made the heavens and the earth, the sea, and all that is in them, but He rested on the seventh day. Therefore the Lord blessed the Sabbath day and made it holy—fails to respect the inspired author's primary intention when arranging God's creative acts in six days. It is a subtle command to take a day of rest. This theological purpose and the ancient poetic structure indicate that Gen 1 is not a historical record of the sequence of actual divine interventions in origins.

The account of the creation of the heavens in Gen 1 provides further evidence that this chapter does not align with the scientific facts. On the second day of creation, God made the firmament and used it to separate the body of waters above from those below. Genesis 1 also states that He placed the sun, moon, and stars in the firmament on the fourth creation day. However, there is no firmament overhead. There is no heavenly sea of water above the earth. And there are no astronomical bodies set in a firmament.[3] Therefore, *since the heavens are not structured in this way, Gen 1 cannot be an account of the actual events that created the heavens.* Scientific concordism fails.

It follows then that if creation days two and four are not a revelation of astronomical origins, then neither are the third, fifth, and sixth days of creation a scientific record of the origin of living organisms. To suggest otherwise is inconsistent. This would rip apart the interwoven creative acts between inanimate structures and living creatures that make up the fabric of Gen 1. The view of origins found in this creation account is based on an ancient phenomenological perspective of the physical world. In the eyes of ancient people, the universe was a static 3-tier structure. It remained the same throughout their lifetime. From their viewpoint, living organisms also appeared to be static, because they never saw plants, animals, or humans change into other forms of life. In attempting to understand the origin of the world, the ancients logically conceived that it was created rapidly and fully formed.

De novo creation is the ancient conception of origins found in the Bible. This term employs the Latin words *de* meaning "from" and *novus* "new." Stated more precisely, it is a view of origins that results in things and beings that are brand new. This type of creative activity is quick and complete. It appears in most ancient creation accounts and it involves a divine being/s who acts rapidly through a series of dramatic interventions, resulting in cosmological structures and living creatures that are mature and fully formed.[4]

Considering the limited scientific evidence available to ancient peoples, this conceptualization of origins was perfectly logical. As with all origins accounts, including those held by us today, the ancients asked basic *etiological* questions (Greek *aitia*: the cause, the reason for this). These included: Where did such-and-such come from? Why is it this way? Who or what is responsible? There was no reason for ancient peoples to believe the universe was billions of years old, and they were unaware of the fossil record, showing that living organisms changed over time. Instead, the age of the world was limited to the lengths of their genealogies, many of which were kept in memory, and therefore quite short. Biological evolution was not even a consideration because in the eyes of the ancients, hens laid eggs that always produced chicks, ewes only gave birth to lambs, and women were invariably the mothers of human infants. Living organisms were therefore static and never changed. In conceptualizing origins, they used these day-to-day experiences and cast them back to the beginning of creation.[5] Ancient peoples came to the reasonable conclusion that the universe and life must have been created quickly and completely formed not very long ago. And this was the best origins science-of-the-day.

Grasping the notion of *de novo* creation is one of the keys to understanding Gen 1 and the origins debate. This creation account refers 10 times to living creatures reproducing "according to its/their kind/s." Young earth creationists and progressive creationists argue that this phrase is solid biblical evidence against biological evolution, because God created separate groups of organisms. They term these groupings "created kinds" or "baramins" (Hebrew *bārā'*: to create; *min*: kind). However, this popular anti-evolutionist belief that the Creator intervened dramatically in the creation of individual groups of plants and animals fails to appreciate the ancient mindset. The phrase "according to its/their kind/s" reflects an ancient phenomenological perspective of living organisms. For example, ancient men and women always saw that birds reproduce birds, which reproduce birds, which reproduce birds, etc. They logically reasoned that there must have been some first or original birds that the Creator had made. Thus, the *de novo* creation of living organisms, such as birds in Gen 1, is based on the classification of life into static categories, as perceived by ancient peoples like the Hebrews. More specifically, it reflects an ancient biology; and in particular, an ancient understanding of taxonomy. This biblical fact has a very challenging implication.

Ancient biology profoundly impacts the conceptualization of the divine acts that created living organisms in Gen 1. Stated precisely, *God's creative action in the origin of life is accommodated through ancient taxonomical categories.* In the same way that Gen 1 filters divine events regarding the origin of the heavens through a 3-tier astronomy and the ancient notion of *de novo* creation (God using the firmament to separate the waters above on creation day two, and His placing of the sun, moon, and stars in the firmament on day four), the phenomenon of seeing living organisms reproduce "according to its/their kind/s" shapes the events regarding the origin of life. The writer of Gen 1 attributes the origin of the basic kinds of plants and animals to *de novo* creative acts by the Creator. In other words, ancient science directs the biblical author's conceptualization of divine creative activity. Ancient peoples saw basic kinds of living organisms around them that never changed, and they reasoned that these creatures must have originally been created quickly and completely formed. It was perfectly logical for them to connect these two notions. We would have come to the same conclusion had we lived at that time. So here's the bottom line: Gen 1 does not reveal how God actually created life.

To be sure, this is challenging and even threatening to most Christians. But the Message-Incident Principle and the principle of accommodation shed light on the situation. In Gen 1, the Holy Spirit descended to the level of the biblical author and his readers, and used their incidental ancient science regarding biological origins to reveal the Message of Faith that He was the Creator of life. The Bible does not lie about how God actually created living organisms; the Bible accommodates and simply does not reveal how He made plants, animals, and . . . humans.

Even though Gen 1 features an ancient phenomenological perspective of origins with no correspondence to physical reality, Christians throughout time have always grasped the basic Messages of Faith: God is the Creator of the world (v. 1), humans have been created in the Image of God (v. 27), and the creation is very good (v. 31). The opening chapter of Scripture also affirms the Sabbath Commandment. The amazing power of the Book of God's Words is that when we are on our knees, the Lord graciously gives us the ability to discover inerrant spiritual truths in Scripture, such as these. Yet the ancient science of origins in Gen 1 has a profound implication: this creation account is not a scientific record of actual events in the origin of the world. Scripture itself unshackles us from the chains of scientific concordism, freeing us to open the Book of God's Works to the chapters dealing specifically with how the Lord made the universe and life.

GENESIS 2: THE CREATION OF ADAM AND EVE

Generations of Christians have firmly believed that the creation of Adam and Eve in Gen 2 is an elaboration of the brief account of human origins on the sixth creation day in Gen 1. This traditional literal interpretation asserts that human history begins with the events in the garden of Eden. According to young earth creationists and progressive creationists, these passages offer indisputable biblical evidence against human evolution. However, conflicts in the order of God's creative acts exist between the first two chapters of Scripture, calling into question the historicity of both accounts. As well, other creation accounts in the ancient Near East reveal that the *de novo* creation of humans was the science-of-the-day, and therefore not historical.

The conflicting order of creative events between Gen 1 and 2 is closely connected to human origins:

Genesis 1		Genesis 2	
vegetation (fruit)	3rd day	man	v. 7
birds	5th day	vegetation (fruit)	v. 8–9
land animals	6th day	land animals & birds	v. 19
man & woman	6th day	woman	v. 22

One of the most glaring problems with the view that Gen 2 offers details on the events of the sixth creation day involves the origin of birds. Genesis 1 states that God created "*every* winged bird according to its kind" (v. 21) on the fifth day, prior to humans; but Gen 2 claims the Lord God formed "*all* the birds of the air" (v. 19) after the man was made. Significantly, both verses use the very same Hebrew adjective (*cōl*: all, every).[6] There is also an inconsistency in the creative order for land animals and humans. Genesis 1 places the origin of "livestock, creatures that move along the ground, and wild animals" (v. 24) before the creation of male and female humans; Gen 2 puts the formation of "*all* [*cōl*] the beasts of the field" (v. 19) in between the fashioning of Adam from dust (v. 7) and Eve from his side (v. 22).[7]

However, these conflicts in the order of creative events between Gen 1 and 2 quickly disappear if we recognize that the Holy Spirit used two different, yet complementary, creation accounts in the revelatory process. The idea that biblical books include different literary sources might be new to some readers, but evidence in Scripture shows that the inspired writers used sources like the Book of the Wars of the Lord (Num 21:14) and the Book of Jashar (Josh 10:11–12; 2 Sam 1:18–27). Distinctive characteristics between Gen 1 and 2 indicate that two different authors composed independent accounts of origins:[8]

	Genesis 1	**Genesis 2**
Literary style	poetry	narrative
	structured & repetitive	free-flowing
Setting of the scene	cosmic/universal	rural/pastoral
Divine name	God	Lord God
Hebrew	*'Ĕlōhîm*	*Yahweh 'Ĕlōhîm*
Creative action	verbal commands	hands-on
Divine Being	transcendent & heavenly	immanent & earthly
Relationship to humans	kingly	personal
Food commands	without a prohibition	with a prohibition
	focus on sustenance	focus on obedience

By placing these two creation accounts side by side, the Bible opens with the revelation that God is both the transcendent Creator of a vast cosmos and the immanent Maker of each and every one of us. The Holy Spirit's intention in juxtaposing Gen 1 and 2 is to disclose the fullness of the Lord's character. And instead of being a problem, conflicts between the creative events in these chapters offer subtle evidence that His purpose was not to reveal *how* He actually created the world, but *that* He created the world.

Like every other account of origins, Gen 2 is etiological. It offers an explanation for the existence of things and beings known to the inspired writer and his readers—vegetation, land animals, birds, and humans. And typical of ancient origins accounts, the Lord God created these *de novo*. Genesis 2 focuses mainly on the origin of humanity. Adam is made "from the dust of the ground" (v. 7). Notably, the use of earth to form a human quickly and completely appears in other ancient Near Eastern creation stories. For example, one account tells of a goddess who mixes clay with the blood of a slain god to fashion seven males and seven females. In another, a drunken divine being uses earth to make imperfect human beings.[9] The gods in many of these pagan accounts create humanity in order to free themselves from work. The message is that men and women are basically slaves of the gods. In sharp contrast, Gen 2 features the Message of Faith that the Lord cares for humanity. He meets their physical and psychological needs by offering food and companionship. The God of Love is being revealed at this early stage of biblical revelation.

So what exactly am I saying about Adam? Yes, the forming of a man from the dust of the ground in Gen 2:7 is an ancient understanding of origins. Adam's existence is based ultimately on ancient science, and his quick and complete creation from earth made perfect sense from an ancient phenomenological perspective. The ancients saw that humans never change into other kinds of creatures, and that humans give birth to humans, who give birth to humans, who give birth to humans, etc. It was reasonable for them to conclude that the Creator had made an original human or pair of humans. In addition, ancient peoples saw that after an organism died, it decomposed and became dust. This observation, coupled with their own activity in shaping clay into pottery, provided a conceptualization for the fashioning of humans from earth. In fact, Gen 2 uses the Hebrew word *yāṣar* to describe the forming of a man, animals, and birds from the ground (v. 7, 8, 19). This is the same word that is used for the term potter, and it even appears in other passages where God is the Potter who forms man in His hands (Isa 16:29, 45:9, 64:8; cf. Jer 18:1–6).

The *de novo* creation of Adam is another example of the Holy Spirit accommodating to the level of the ancient Hebrews. He takes their view of human origins, which was the best science-of-the-day, and employs it to reveal that He is their Creator. And just like His use of ancient astronomy when He separates the waters above from the waters below with the firmament, His forming of Adam from dust never happened either. No doubt about it, this idea is shocking to most Christians. But again, *how* God made humans is incidental to the message *that* He made us. Adam is simply an ancient vessel that delivers eternal truths about our spiritual condition.

The main purpose of Gen 2 is to reveal inerrant Messages of Faith about humanity. Radically different from the pagan beliefs of the nations surrounding the Hebrews, this chapter complements the Divine Theology of Gen 1 and asserts that humans are a unique and privileged creation. We are the only creatures in a personal relationship with the Lord. The second creation account in Scripture also discloses that men and women were made to enjoy the mystery of marriage. So beautifully stated, "A man will leave his father and mother and be united to his wife, and they will become one flesh" (v. 24). And most importantly, Gen 2 reveals that the Creator sets limits on human freedom. He commands Adam, "You must not eat from the tree of the knowledge of good and evil, for when you eat of it you shall surely die" (v. 17). We are accountable before God, and failure to respect His commands has serious consequences.

GENESIS 3: THE FALL

The church throughout time has tenaciously defended that the fall of Adam and Eve in the garden of Eden is a historical fact. As punishment for his sin, the Lord condemns Adam to suffer in life and then to die.* God also curses the ground. The New Testament aligns with the traditional literal reading of the events in Gen 3. The apostle Paul states directly, "Death came through a man" (1 Cor 15:20), and "Sin entered the world through one man, and death through sin" (Rom 5:12). As well, Paul accepts the cosmic fall. He claims that "the whole creation has been groaning" because it "was subjected to frustration" and placed "in bondage to decay" (Rom 8:20–22). However, Gen 3 is rooted deeply in an ancient understanding of origins that points away from the events being historical. In addition, the fossil pattern in the geological record demonstrates that human sin did not lead to the entrance of suffering and death into the world.

Genesis 3 is built on the notion embraced by many ancient peoples that the world was originally harmonious, but this idyllic age was lost.[10] Belief in an original paradise is clearly seen in both the first (Gen 1) and second (Gen 2) biblical creation accounts.[11] The idea of an idyllic environment also appears in other ancient Near East literature. One story describes a land that is "pure," "clean," and "bright" where "the lion does not kill, the wolf does not plunder the lamb" and "old men do not say, 'I am an old man.'"[12] However, in many of these accounts, the harmonious age was lost and led to the present world with its hardships and afflictions. Notably, the deterioration of the original creation is often the result of humans being punished by the gods.

Belief in a lost idyllic age is perfectly logical from an ancient phenomenological perspective. Ancient peoples experienced numerous afflictions and struggles, and they rationally concluded that there must be a cause for these phenomena. Their attempt to find an etiology for the bad things around them was no different than that of explaining the origin of the firmament above them. Just as they had conceived that the hard dome overhead had entered the world abruptly through a dramatic divine

---

* It must be underlined that Gen 3 does not refer to spiritual death, as progressive creationists claim. Verse 19 definitely deals with physical death because in judging Adam the Lord states, "For dust you are and to dust you will return." Also see pages 141–43.

intervention, so too was the entrance of troubles and hardships at one point in the past. A corollary (logical deduction) of this ancient reasoning is that prior to the introduction of adversities, the world was in a happier and more harmonious state. For the inspired author of Gen 3, the harsh realities of birth pangs (v. 16), sweaty and painful work (v. 17, 19), thistles and thorns (v. 18), and ultimately death (v. 19), all pointed back to the loss of an original utopian creation.

More specifically, the ancient Hebrew writer, under the guidance of the Holy Spirit, understood the cause for the lost idyllic age to be human sin and God judging this sin. In other words, Gen 3 uses an ancient concept often found in origins accounts as a vessel to reveal an inerrant spiritual truth. No doubt about it, this is a very challenging idea to grasp. Yet once more, the ancient astronomy in Scripture offers insight. As noted in the previous chapter, the Bible states that at the final judgment God will first shake the firmament, causing the stars to fall to the earth, and then He will roll up this heavenly structure (Isa 34:4; Matt 24:27, 29). But obviously, this is not how the world will end, because there is no starry firmament above us. The dismantling of the 3-tier universe at the end of time is an incidental vessel that delivers a revelation about divine judgment. In other words, God's judgmental action at the end of the world is accommodated through ancient astronomical categories.

In a similar way, Gen 3 uses the ancient notion of a lost idyllic age to reveal the same critical Message of Faith—God judges humans for their sins. Stated more precisely, *the Lord's judgmental action in the garden of Eden account is accommodated through the ancient notion that an idyllic age was lost*. In particular, Gen 3 features an ancient science of origins regarding the entrance of suffering and death into the world. However, like the dismantling of the heavens in Scripture, it is not a revelation about how these harsh physical realities actually originated. Instead, the Holy Spirit accommodated and used the writer's ancient understanding of the origin of suffering and death as a vessel to reveal that He judges human sin.

So what exactly am I saying now? That's right, the events in Gen 3 did not happen as stated. There never was a cosmic fall. This biblical chapter is a something-went-wrong-in-the-world account. It is etiological and answers the question: Where did death, suffering, and other terrible things come from? Even more importantly: How did sin enter the world? It makes perfect sense that the Holy Spirit used the scientific notions-of-the-day, like the *de novo* creation of humanity and the lost idyllic age. These concepts were foundations of the ancient view of nature, and utiliz-

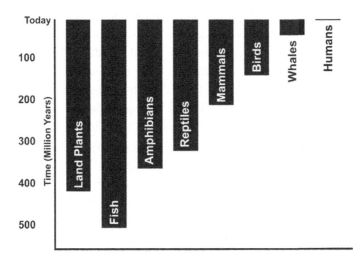

Fig 4-3. The Pattern of Fossils in the Geological Record. For the sake of simplicity, the animals presented in this diagram are limited to vertebrates (back-boned animals) and those referred or alluded to in Gen 1 and 2. This is also the case with plants being restricted to only land plants.

ing them facilitated biblical revelation. Thus, the Message of Faith in Gen 3 is not dependent upon the historical reality of Adam or the loss of an idyllic garden in Eden. Instead, these ancient ideas about the origin of humans and physical adversities are incidental to a Divine Theology that was radically different from the pagan beliefs surrounding the Hebrews.

Genesis 3 reveals the reality, manifestation, and consequence of human sin. It offers a penetrating picture of our spiritual condition. Even though Adam and Eve were tempted by evil, they freely and deliberately chose to disobey God. This chapter is also a revelation of reactions and responses to being caught in sin. After eating the forbidden fruit, the first couple are ashamed and afraid, and try hiding from the Lord. When confronted by Him, they rationalize their sinfulness. Eve blames the snake, and Adam blames his wife. In fact, Adam places the ultimate responsibility for his transgression on the Creator! Amazingly, he complains that it was "the woman *You* put here with me" that led him into sin (v. 12; my italics). However, the Message of Faith in Gen 3 is that humans are responsible for their actions and they are accountable before God. The consequences of disobedience are significant because the Creator judges men and women for their sins.

Modern science also assists us in determining whether or not Gen 3 is historical. Fig 4-3 sketches the pattern of fossils found in the crust of the earth. Notably, this pattern has been known for more than 150 years. In fact, the basic outline was established around 1850 by a majority of geologists who were devout Christians, and it pre-dates Darwin's famed book on biological evolution, *On the Origin of Species* (1859). In other words, the geological record was formulated by anti-evolutionists. Today, Christian leaders in the origins debate rarely question the integrity of the fossil pattern in the earth's crust, because it is there in front of their eyes, plain to see. An advantage of this scientific evidence is that it is within reach for most people and does not require specialized knowledge. We can all understand its basic truths, just like any professional geologist.

The pattern of fossils in the geological record reveals, without any doubt whatsoever, that suffering and death existed in the world well before the appearance of humans on earth. And using standard geological dates for the age of the earth, it is indisputable that biological pain and mortality preceded humans by 100s of millions of years. If there was a connection between the sin of Adam and physical death as stated in Gen 3, then the fossil pattern predicted by young earth creation would be found (Fig 4-5; page 88). Human remains would appear at the lowest level along with the bones of every life form ever created. Clearly, human sin is not connected to the origin of suffering and death in the world. The cosmic fall never happened. Once again, scientific concordism fails.

The modern geological record and the ancient notion of a lost idyllic age indicate that Gen 3 is not a historical account. The implications of this conclusion are far reaching. They directly call into question traditional belief in the existence and fall of Adam and Eve. Concerns are also raised about the apostle Paul's literal reading of this chapter as seen in Rom 5 and 8 and 1 Cor 15. And the traditional doctrine of original sin, which is based on the assumption that the garden of Eden account is historical, appears suspect. More will be said about these critical issues in chapters 6 and 7.

Even though most Christians read Gen 3 as actual history, the power of this divinely inspired account has been affirmed over and over again throughout the ages. It has consistently convicted men and women of their sins, and has left them knowing that God judges them. Genesis 3 is our personal story. Who has not experienced the spiritual realities in the garden of Eden? Is anyone not tempted to disobey the words of their Maker? Ever wanted to hide because of a sinful act? And who has not tried to rationalize their sin before the Holy Spirit? In order to understand our life, we must see ourselves in the garden—Adam and Eve are you and me.

ANCIENT ACCOUNT OF ORIGINS INSPIRED BY GOD

Let's sum up these three sections on Gen 1–3. Similar to origins accounts both past and present, the opening chapters of Scripture are etiological. Genesis 1 answers certain questions: Where did the heavens, earth, and life come from? Who or what is responsible for their origin? Genesis 2 is more specific and deals directly with the creation of humans. And Gen 3 is an explanation and justification for the presence of harsh realities in the world—sin, suffering, and death. Like all other ancient and modern accounts of origins, Gen 1–3 features both metaphysical and physical statements.

First and foremost, the creation week, the creation of Adam and Eve, and the fall are the Holy Spirit-inspired Word of God. The purpose of these chapters is to reveal metaphysical truths; more specifically, a Divine Theology. The Messages of Faith include foundational beliefs of Christianity: (1) the God of the Bible created the universe and life, (2) the world is a very good creation, (3) men and women are the only creatures made in the Image of God, (4) every person has fallen into sin, and (5) God judges humans for their sinful acts. All committed Christians embrace these inerrant spiritual truths. As far as I'm concerned, these are non-negotiable beliefs.

Second, Gen 1–3 features an ancient science regarding the origin of the physical world. It was the best science-of-the-day a few thousand years ago. Similar to us today, the ancient Hebrews looked at the world around them, and then attempted to understand how it came into existence. This is the same type of thinking that police use in crime scene investigations. They take the present physical evidence and attempt to reconstruct the past. Of course, we have the advantage of much more scientific data like fossil patterns in the geological record. Nevertheless, God's chosen people saw a static 3-tier universe and static living organisms. From their ancient phenomenological perspective, they conceived that the universe and life were put together quickly and completely formed. The idea of *de novo* creation was perfectly logical. In addition, the ancient Hebrews experienced harsh realities like sin, suffering, and death. They knew that sinfulness was the greatest problem plaguing the world. To believe in the lost idyllic age and a cosmic fall from an original creation, and to connect these to human sin and divine judgment, was completely rational. Even today, many people view terrible events as God's judgment on immoral behavior.

GEN 1-3

MESSAGE
Divine Theology
God created the world
The world is very good
Humans created in Image of God
Humans are sinful
God judges humans for sin

INCIDENT
Ancient Science of Origins
De novo creation of the world
Lost idyllic age
Origin of death
Cosmic fall
Ancient Literature
Ancient poetry
Ancient sources

Fig 4-4. Genesis 1–3: Divine Theology and Ancient Features

Finally, the first three chapters of Scripture are ancient literature, characterised by ancient poetry and ancient sources. In other words, the Holy Spirit accommodated by using the literary techniques-of-the-day. Genesis 1 is built on parallel panels and the Hebrew work week and Sabbath. Genesis 1–3 includes two sources. A close examination of these opening chapters reveals conflicts and contradictions in the order of the creative events. For example, light appears before the creation of the sun in Gen 1; birds are created before the male and female humans in Gen 1, but after the man and before the woman in Gen 2. Instead of viewing these biblical facts as a threat to our faith, these features in the Word of God are subtle signposts pointing us away from the assumption that Gen 1–3 is a historical record of actual events in the origin of the universe and life. That is, the Bible itself is offering internal evidence against scientific concordism. And I believe that we should submit our understanding of origins to this scriptural data.

Fig 4-4 summarizes the features of Gen 1–3 mentioned above in light of the Message-Incident Principle. These opening biblical chapters are *an ancient account of origins, written by the early Hebrews and inspired by the Holy Spirit*. To reveal an inerrant Divine Theology as effectively as possible, God descended to the level of the ancient Hebrews and used their ancient understanding of science and their ancient techniques of literature. In the same way that the Lord meets us wherever we happen to be, He accommodated in order to reveal Himself and His will in the first three chapters of Scripture.

Finally, as an evolutionary creationist, I am often asked whether God lied in the Bible. Let me make this very clear one more time: GOD DID NOT LIE IN THE BIBLE. Instead, as a loving Father, He accommodated to the level of His chosen people, the Hebrews. Jesus did the same in taking on human flesh and descending to our level. Genesis 1–3 was written thousands of years ago, and as a result, today we must not conflate, but rather separate the life-giving Messages of Faith from the incidental ancient science of origins. In this way, we can draw spiritual nourishment from its ancient vessel and enjoy a personal relationship with our Creator.

FOSSIL PATTERN PREDICTIONS

Scientific concordism is a foundational principle in young earth creation and progressive creation. Both positions assume that the Holy Spirit revealed scientific facts to the biblical writers thousands of years before their discovery by modern science. Consequently, it is possible to make scientific predictions based on these anti-evolutionary views, and to test them against the scientific evidence. As noted earlier, Christian leaders in the origins debate today accept the geological record and the arrangement of fossils in the crust of the earth. Using the living organisms mentioned or implied in Gen 1 and 2, we can compare the fossil patterns predicted by the anti-evolutionary origins positions with the actual fossil pattern in the geological record (Fig 4-3; page 84).

Fig 4-5 presents the fossil pattern prediction of young earth creation. This view of origins asserts that the universe and life were created as described by a strict literal reading of Gen 1. Soon afterwards, sin entered the world, and so too the physical death of humans and other living organisms. Thus, at the bottom of the geological record there should be the remains of every creature that God made during the creation week, including all extinct animals. Notably, one would expect to find dinosaurs (which are reptiles) and humans together at the base of the fossil record. Thus, scientific creationism predicts a "creation basal layer." Even assuming the young earth creationist belief in Noah's global flood, this evidence would remain in the bottom geological layer because of one simple fact: bones and teeth do not float. However, it is obvious that the fossil pattern

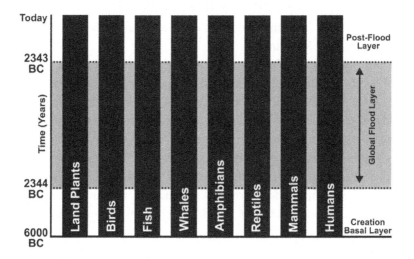

Fig 4-5. Young Earth Creation Fossil Pattern Prediction. The dates for the creation of the world (6000 BC) and the flood of Noah (2344 BC) are determined by adding the lifespan of individuals that appear in genealogies of the Bible.

predicted by young earth creation does not even come close to the actual geological facts (Fig 4-3).

Twenty-five years ago, I fiercely defended the young earth creationist interpretation of Noah's flood and the geological record. It is a scientific fact that most of the layers (strata) and fossils in the earth's crust were laid down in water. The parallel strata in the earth's crust indicate this is the case. But a closer examination of the fossil pattern prediction based on a worldwide deluge reveals an insurmountable problem. Noah's flood would have produced a "global flood layer" with strata featuring the mixing of bones and teeth of every animal ever created. In fact, depending on the turbulence of the deluge, gravity should have placed heavier bones (e.g., dinosaurs, elephants) near the bottom of the flood layer and lighter ones at the top. But no such fossil pattern exists in the crust of the earth. Instead, the geological record presents a very consistent pattern, with the sequential appearance of fish first, amphibians next, then reptiles, and mammals last, with humans the latest.

There are other serious problems with young earth creation not presented in Fig 4-5. The first fish were jawless and they appeared about 500 million years ago (mya). About 100 million years later, fish with jaws and teeth are found in the fossil record. As most people know, sharks have teeth

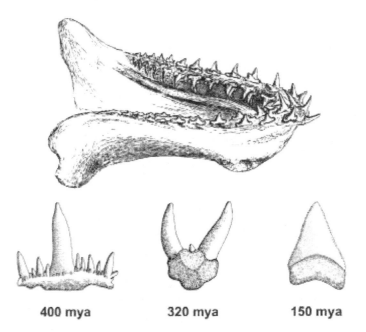

400 mya   **320 mya**   **150 mya**

Fig 4-6. Shark Jaw and Teeth. Rows of teeth develop inside of the mouth and move to the outside of the jaw where they are shed continually (top). Like a fingerprint, each species of shark has a distinct tooth anatomy. The fossil record presents layers of strata marked by different teeth indicative of the evolution of sharks (bottom). The tooth on the far right is that of a Great White Shark. mya: million years ago. Single shark teeth redrawn by Braden Barr.

that are shed throughout their lifetime (Fig 4-6). Creation science, then, predicts that shark teeth should be scattered across the original ocean floor; in other words, at the very lowest levels of the marine fossil record. But incalculable numbers of these teeth only appear after 400 mya.

Similarly, dinosaurs like the famed T-Rex continuously replace teeth during their lifetime (Fig 4-7). However, this reptile and its countless shed teeth are confined to a narrow region that is relatively high in the geological record, between 85 and 65 mya. A world created *de novo* 6000 years ago should have the remains of T-Rex along with every other plant and animal ever made, including humans, at the base of the fossil record (i.e., in the creation basal layer). But this prediction does not align with the scientific facts.

Finally, land plants appear about 420 mya. Many of these release millions of microscopic pollen grains during their reproductive cycle (they are a common cause of allergies today). In a young earth creationist world, all plants were made on the third day of creation. Therefore, we

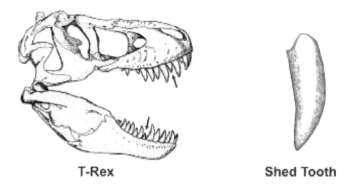

T-Rex   Shed Tooth

Fig 4-7. *Tyrannosaurus Rex* **Skull and Teeth.** Spaces in the dental row indicate the loss of a tooth. Replacement teeth later erupt into the gaps (arrows). The shed tooth of T-Rex (right) is over 6 inches long and does not have a root, because it was resorbed by tissues of the underlying and developing replacement tooth. Notably, these teeth only appear in the fossil record between 85–65 million years ago. They are designed to puncture and slash flesh, offering clear evidence that death was in the world well before humans appeared. See also Fig 5-3; page 101. Skull courtesy of Tracy Ford; tooth drawn by Braden Barr.

should expect to find every type of pollen in every layer of the earth's crust. But we don't. Fruit-bearing (flowering) plants should also appear throughout the fossil record. However, they are only found near the top of geological strata, after 130 mya. To summarize, it is quite clear that scientific creationism does not align with the scientific evidence.

Fig 4-8 outlines the fossil pattern prediction of progressive creation. This position claims that Gen 1 offers a historical outline of God's creative acts over eons of time, and that the creation "days" represent geological epochs of 100s of millions of years. However, obvious inversions exist in the fossil order between the progressive creationist prediction and the scientific facts. Geological evidence demonstrates that fish appeared more than 400 million years before fruit trees. However, Scripture states that trees, including those that bear fruit, were created on the third creation day/age and fish on the fifth. Similarly, Gen 1 places the origin of land animals after the appearance of birds and marine creatures. But the fossil record indicates that terrestrial animals like reptiles arose nearly 200 million years before the first birds and about 300 million years before whales, which are one of the "great creatures of the sea" (v. 21). Finally, Gen 1 states that botanical life was created one day before the sun. Yet without

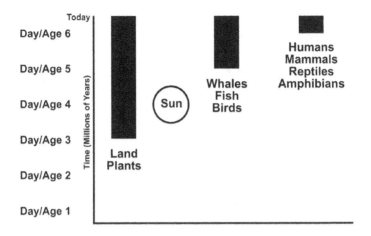

Fig 4-8. Progressive Creation Fossil Pattern Prediction

sunlight, plants and trees would not have been able to reproduce "according to their kinds" (v. 12) over millions of years during the third day/age.

A few comments need to be made regarding the handling of Scripture by progressive creationists. In order to justify 100s of millions of years of death in the geological record before the appearance of human fossils, they attempt to argue that the sin of Adam in Gen 3 did not result in physical death entering the world, but only spiritual death. However, this is not what the Bible says. In Gen 3:19, God condemns Adam to die physically by stating, "For dust you are, and to dust you shall return."

Day-age creationists also claim that Noah's flood is local, supposedly in a region of the Middle East, such as the Mesopotamian plain between the Tigris and Euphrates Rivers. But again, this betrays Scripture. Genesis 8:4–5 indicates that the waters covered the tops of the Ararat Mountains, which are over 16,000 feet high. Clearly, the Noahic deluge was not a local flood according to the Bible.[13] In addition, I find that the progressive creationist interpretation of the flood defies common sense. If the flood was local, why didn't humans and animals simply move to higher ground as they do today when rivers flood?

Lastly, progressive creationists interpret the word "day" in Gen 1 as a period that is 100s of millions of years long in order to harmonize Scripture with the age of the universe offered by modern science. To defend their position, they often appeal to 2 Pet 3:8, "With the Lord a day is like a thousand years, and a thousand years are like a day." However, every

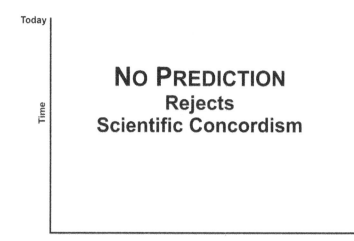

Fig 4-9. Evolutionary Creation

time the Hebrew word day (*yōm*) appears in the Old Testament with a number, such as in Gen 1, it refers to a regular 24-hour day. In addition, Gen 1 even describes the length of each creation day with the concluding statement: "There was evening and there was morning—the first [second, third, etc.] day." Thus, the days of creation are 24-hour periods, and not geological or cosmological epochs. In sum, the progressive creationist interpretation of the opening chapter of Scripture is unbiblical.

Fig 4-9 presents evolutionary creation. In contrast to young earth creation and progressive creation, this conservative Christian origins position rejects scientific concordism. It makes no fossil pattern prediction based on the Bible, because Scripture features ancient science. To do otherwise would be like using the firmament and waters above in modern astronomy. Or put in practical terms, it would be similar to NASA scientists using the biblical understanding of the heavens to launch spacecraft. Evolutionary creationists assert that biological evolution is one of the easiest theories to disprove. If only one fossil is out of order in the geological record, then this scientific theory collapses. For example, the discovery of a human tooth in the strata of the dinosaurs would destroy the theory completely. To date, there has never been a fossil out of place. And considering the incalculable number of fossils that have been discovered, I doubt any will ever be found.

This chapter affirms Billy Graham's statement in the epigraph at the front of this book: "The Bible is not a book of science." Genesis 1–3 features an ancient understanding of origins. Consequently, it is not possible to align Scripture with science. In fact, the Bible itself reveals that scientific concordism fails. Of course, this is a new and challenging idea for most Christians. But it does not pose any problem for our faith if we remember that the Holy Spirit accommodated to the level of the ancient Hebrews when He inspired the biblical accounts of origins. Therefore, as we read Gen 1–3, we must separate the life-changing Messages of Faith from the ancient science. In this way, Christians are freed from scientific concordism and allowed to open without fear the Book of God's Works to the chapters dealing with the age of the earth and the origin of life. We now turn to examine some of this exciting scientific evidence.

5

Evidence for an Old Earth and Evolution

I BECAME A CHRISTIAN by reading the gospel of John while serving as a United Nations peacekeeper on the island of Cyprus. Upon my return home to Canada, the Lord led me to a wonderful evangelical church that focused on Scripture and living a holy lifestyle. Having had a university education in science, I needed to answer the question of origins. I was just like the high school student that I mentioned in the preface of this book. He wanted to know how dinosaurs fit into the Bible, and so did I. But like most in my church, I was trapped in the origins dichotomy. Being a Christian meant rejecting evolution. And it was not long before I was introduced to books written by young earth creationists. With unreserved confidence, they declared that there was not a shred of evidence that the earth was old or that life had evolved. I immersed myself in this literature, and I soon accepted the belief embraced by many born-again Christians that "Satan himself is the originator of the concept of evolution."[1]

Looking back on that period in my life, I now realize that I was missing a lot of information. I was oblivious to the fact that the Bible has an ancient science. Since my education was in the sciences, my natural tendency was to read Scripture as if it was a book of science. And though I had training in biology, it was mainly in scientific disciplines (anatomy, physiology, pathology, dentistry) that did not have much to do with biological evolution or the age of the earth. Therefore, when young earth creationists in my church assured me that there was no evidence whatsoever for evolution or an old earth, I trusted them, and I believed them. And because of them, I eventually left my career as a dentist with the intention of becoming a creation scientist in order to attack universities and their brainwashing of students with the satanic lie of evolution.

However, as we have seen so far in this book, Scripture contains ancient science and an ancient understanding of origins. Scientific concordism fails. The fossil pattern predictions of young earth creation and progressive creation also fail. This being the case, an interesting possibility emerges. Far from originating from Satan, the evolutionary sciences may well be similar to other sciences, the benefits of which we enjoy every day, like medicine and engineering. In other words, cosmology, geology, and evolutionary biology might be good gifts from the Father (Matt 7:11) that reveal to us how He actually created the universe and life. But in order to understand the origin of His creation, we need to open the Book of God's Works to the chapters dealing specifically with the age of the earth and biological evolution.

This chapter is a very modest introduction to some basic scientific evidence for an old earth and evolution. I have chosen examples that require no specialized scientific training to understand and that challenge the Christian anti-evolutionary positions. First, I will offer physical data that confirms the earth is much older than a few thousand years, and then introduce some transitional fossils of creatures that were in the process of changing into new forms of life. I will also present genetic and molecular features found in living organisms today that point back to their evolutionary past. Of course, those familiar with the overwhelming evidence that supports an old earth and evolution know that such an outline hardly scratches the surface. Yet in drawing this sketch, my hope is that Christians who are skeptical of the evolutionary sciences will be encouraged to open the Book of Nature to see this amazing and God-glorifying evidence.

AGE OF THE EARTH

The age of the earth continues to be a controversial issue in a number of churches today. Young earth creationists contend that the belief in a 6,000 year-old world is biblical, and even essential to Christian faith. They calculate this age by adding up the genealogies in Scripture. Creation scientists also claim that most of the layers of stratification in the crust of the earth, as seen in the sides of canyons and mountains, were deposited in one year, during Noah's flood. However, geologists rejected these ideas more than 250 years ago. This section offers a few basic facts on why young earth creationist views are not even considered within the scientific community.[2]

One way to understand the age of the earth and geological stratification is to view the crust of the earth like pieces of paper that collect over time in an in-basket. Layers of paper at the bottom of the basket were the first "strata" to be deposited. These are "older" than the "younger" sheets of paper near the top, since the latter were put in at a later time. Occasionally a piece of paper has a temporal reference, such as the date on a bill or a letter. These "age markers" on different documents function like "clocks" and reveal the approximate time when paper strata were laid down in the basket. Therefore, it is possible to reconstruct the "stratification history" of the papers and even to offer dates as to when some were placed. A top-to-bottom pattern results with the "ages" of the paper strata increasing progressively as we go down into the basket. The earth features similar layering and time markers.

Layers Deposited on Earth

There are countless layers of different materials found everywhere on earth. The most prominent are rock strata, like those in the walls of the Grand Canyon and the sides of the Rocky Mountains. Layering also appears with sediments laid down in water, deposits excreted by living organisms, and seasonal accumulations of snow. The significance of these three examples is that they deal with layers that are being deposited today. As a result, we can measure the rate of deposition of each layer, and then calculate the age of the lowest layer by simply counting the number of layers. Similarly, measuring the thickness of all the layers can determine the amount of time it took to form them. These three simple examples demonstrate that the earth is a great deal older than 6,000 years.

First, the bottoms of lakes have yearly accumulations. Known as "varves," these layers appear as a pair of dark and light bands. The former is sediment deposited during the fall/winter, and the latter in the spring/summer. Varves can number in the tens to hundreds of thousands. Notably, the Green River Formation in the Western United States features the bottom of an ancient lake that no longer exists. It averages 2000 feet in thickness and in some places has more than one million annual varves.

Second, coral reefs are made up of limestone that is laid down by the coral animals. These deposits also have layers of yearly banding. The rate of accumulation is known to be between 5 and 8 millimeters per year, and measuring the thickness of a reef can determine its approximate age. In the Pacific Ocean, the Eniwetok reef is more than 4,500 feet thick and estimated to be at least 200,000 years old.

Third, polar ice sheets feature tens of thousands of annual snow layers. There is no sunlight in this region during the winter, and consequently no daily evaporation occurs on the surface layer of snow. This produces dense and fine-grained snow crystals that appear as a dark band. In the summer, snow is warmed during the day and cooled at night, resulting in a light-colored layer with low density, coarse-grained crystals. The Greenland ice sheet is over two miles thick in some areas and has yearly bands revealing that it is more than 100,000 years old.

The power of these three examples of naturally occurring layers on the earth is that they are independent of each other. The first involves seasonal runoff in freshwater lakes, the second excretions from tropical saltwater organisms, and the third snowfall in a polar region. In other words, this scientific evidence acts like three completely different clocks (e.g., digital, spring wound, and hour glass), and they all indicate that the age of the earth is much, much older than 6,000 years.

Time Markers and Radiometric Dating

The crust of the earth has numerous time markers that are used to calculate the age of its layers of stratification. These "clocks" are made up of unstable atoms that change into other atoms at a constant rate. This natural process is known as "radioactive decay." It is the basic principle behind the scientific techniques used to demonstrate that the earth is billions of years old. Regrettably, radiometric dating is another issue that creates controversy in many churches.

A simple analogy introduces the basic concept behind this method of determining the age of the earth. Imagine three new candles, each made with a different type of wax that burns at a different rate. They are lit at the same time and placed in a room. After an unknown period of time, the candles are extinguished simultaneously and the wax drippings are collected from each. Then they are relit to determine how much time it takes to produce the same amount of dripping for every candle. Even though the candles burn at different rates, and a different amount of wax drips from each, the length of time that they were burning in the room can still be calculated. In this example, the three independent candle "clocks" will give the identical "date" for when they began to "decay."

Radioactive atoms are unstable and naturally decay into other atoms. The rate of change is measurable and it is found to be constant. The measurement of change is known as a "half-life," which is defined as the amount

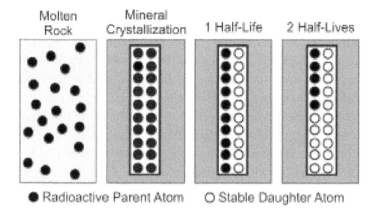

Fig 5-1. Radioactive Decay and Half-Lives. As molten rock hardens (shaded area), minerals crystallize (inner box) and some trap radioactive atoms. Different minerals feature unique internal structures, allowing only certain atoms to fit inside them. At the time of crystallization, a mineral will have 100% radioactive parent atoms and 0% stable daughter atoms. After every half-life, one-half of the radioactive atoms in a mineral will have changed into stable atoms.

of time it takes for half of the radioactive atoms in a sample to change into another type of atom (Fig 5-1). For example, a radioactive form of potassium turns into the gas argon and has a half-life of 1,300,000,000 years. That is, it takes 1.3 billion years for half of the former to become the latter; this same amount of time for half of the remaining potassium to change into more argon; and another 1.3 billion years for another reduction in half of the diminishing potassium in the sample, etc. In other words, the number of potassium atoms in the original sample reduces by 1/2, 1/4, 1/8, etc. Therefore, knowing the ratio of potassium-to-argon in a rock can determine its age. High amounts of potassium indicate a young age, while low amounts an old age (or vice versa using the amount of argon).

Potassium-argon dating is particularly effective with volcanic ash layers. The extreme temperatures in volcanoes expel argon gas, so when certain minerals in the ash cool and crystallize, only potassium is incorporated. In this way, the potassium-argon clock is set back to "0." That is, these minerals contain 0% argon and 100% potassium. As strata in the earth's crust accumulate over time, ash layers are also laid down, and therefore it is possible to calculate their ages by measuring the potassium-to-argon ratio. In addition, other radioactive atoms are found in geological strata. Different forms of uranium change into certain types of lead at very slow rates, similar to potassium and argon. These often appear in lava

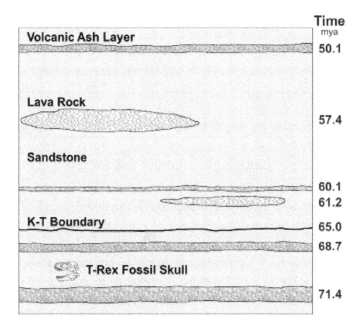

Fig 5-2. Radiometric Dating and Geological Stratification. The age of rocks dated with radioactive methods progressively increases as the depth increases. Different radiometric clocks provide similar dates for strata near the same level, such as the ash layer (61.0 mya) and lava rock (61.2 mya) in the middle of the diagram. Objects that cannot be dated directly are assigned an age within a range. For example, the age of the T-Rex skull is between 68.7 and 71.4 million years old. A distinct geological layer, termed "the K-T Boundary," is found throughout the world and marks the mass extinction of two-thirds of plants and animals, including the dinosaurs. See also Fig 5-3. mya: millions of years ago. Drawn by Braden Barr.

flows. As the molten rock cools and hardens, certain minerals incorporate only uranium as they crystallize. Thus, the radiometric clock is reset to "0" for lead, allowing the rock to be dated. The power of the potassium/argon and uranium/lead dating methods is that they are independent of each other and provide ages that are consistent through the geological record. It must be noted that there are several other radioactive atoms that are used for dating the earth, and they provide similar results. Fig 5-2 illustrates the radiometric dating of strata.

Finally, a comment needs to be made with regard to another radiometric dating method—carbon-14. Many Christians assume that this technique is used to determine the age of the earth. Not true. Carbon-14 is a radioactive atom that decays into carbon-12. However, its half-life is quite short, only about 5700 years. After 10 half-lives, just a small fraction

(1/1024) of these atoms in the original sample remains, making accurate calculations very difficult. Therefore, the upper limit of this dating method is around 50,000 years. In contrast, potassium/argon and uranium/lead have half-lives that are over 1,000,000,000 years, and these are more suitable for calculating the age of the earth. But C-14 is an excellent tool in determining younger ages, like those of bones and wooden artifacts found at archaeological sites. It is routinely used in biblical archaeology.

Geological Column and Timetable

The layers in the crust of the earth are characterized by their contents, allowing scientists to map out a geological column and timetable (Fig 5-3). Different strata feature different types of plant and animal fossils, and a progressive pattern exists, from simple life forms near the bottom to more complex ones at the top. Independent time markers are also found in geological layers. The ages of the strata decrease from the bottom (highest age) to the top (lowest age) and these reflect the sequential depositing of radiometric materials over time.

Young earth creationists claim that most of the layers in the earth's crust were laid down in one year during Noah's flood, which they contend was global. However, two simple features in the geological column and timetable reveal the problem with this anti-evolutionary belief.

First, a worldwide flood would produce strata that contain a mixture of all living organisms. But the scientific facts reveal an orderly progression in the appearance of life forms indicative of evolution. The pattern for fossil plants shows: single cells ⇨ marine plants ⇨ land plants ⇨ seed bearing plants ⇨ flowering plants. A similar progression appears with animals: single cells ⇨ soft-bodied marine animals ⇨ marine animals with skeletons ⇨ jawless fish ⇨ jawed fish ⇨ amphibians ⇨ reptiles ⇨ mammals ⇨ primates ⇨ pre-humans ⇨ humans. To date, science has yet to find *one* fossil plant or animal in the earth's crust that is outside this pattern in the geological column.

Second, a year long global flood would have produced geological layers with radiometrically datable materials mixed together. In other words, the crust of the earth would never feature strata with a progressive sequence of ages across 100s of millions of years. However, the geological record presents a consistent time pattern that decreases from 4 billion years at its lowest levels to the highest strata today with zero age. Significantly, there is not *one* layer in the crust of the earth with radioac-

Era	Period	Age Million Years	1st Fossil Evidence
CENOZOIC	Quaternary		Humans
		2	Archeological Artifacts Pre-Humans
	Tertiary		Whales, Primates
		65	Extinction of Dinosaurs
MESOZOIC	Cretaceous	144	Flowering Plants Birds
	Jurassic		
		208	
	Triassic		Mammals, Dinosaurs
		245	
PALEOZOIC	Permian		
		286	
	Carboniferous		Reptiles, Seed Bearing Plants
		360	
	Devonian		Amphibians
		408	Jawed Fishes Land Plants
	Silurian		
		438	
	Ordovician		
		505	Jawless Fishes
	Cambrian		Marine Animals with Skeletons
		570	
PRECAMBRIAN	Proterozoic		Soft-Bodied Marine Animals Marine Plants
		2500	
	Archean		Single Cell Life
		4600	Origin of Earth

Fig 5-3. The Geological Column and Timetable. Geological periods are often defined by dramatic differences in the fossil record, such as between the Cretaceous and Tertiary, dated at 65 million years ago. Two-thirds of plants and animals disappeared, including the dinosaurs. These two periods are separated by a unique geological layer, the K-T Boundary, which features 20 to 30 times the normal level of iridium (see Fig 5-2). This rare element is common in asteroids. Evidence of a 125 mile-wide impact site on the Yucatan Peninsula in Mexico indicates that an asteroid impact contributed to this mass extinction.

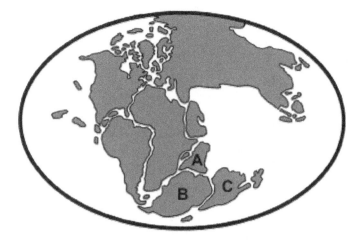

Fig 5-4. Reconstruction of Pangaea. The drift of continents explains the observation made by most people that the coast of South America matches that of Africa like pieces of a jigsaw puzzle. Plate tectonics also accounts for the origin of mountain ranges. For example, India (A) traveled northward and collided with Asia, creating the Himalayan Mountains. (B) Antarctica (C) Australia

tive deposits that is outside this bottom-to-top pattern in age reduction as described by the geological timetable.

The Mid-Atlantic Ridge

Let me offer one last example that I find to be fascinating evidence for an extremely old earth. The surface of the earth is made up of seven massive plates: the North American, South American, Eurasian, African, Australian, Antarctic, and Pacific plates. There are also a number of smaller plates. Through a geological process known as "continental drift" or "plate tectonics," these plates move very slowly, at an average rate of roughly five centimeters a year. Some spread apart, resulting in regions where the seafloor widens, while others converge and can lead to the formation of mountains. Most people living in California are aware that contact between the Pacific and North American plates causes earthquakes in their state.

In the middle of the Atlantic Ocean, the seafloor is spreading apart in a region called "the Mid-Atlantic Ridge." The North and South American plates moving west, and the Eurasian and African plates shifting east cause this. Remarkably, if the direction of these plates is reversed, the continents

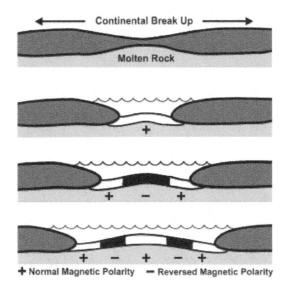

Fig 5-5. Sea Floor Expansion. As the rift between continents widens, molten rock from the core of the earth rises and hardens to fill the gap. The new sea floor is magnetized according the earth's magnetic field at that point in time. In other words, the sea floor is similar to a magnetic tape recorder in that it records magnetic field reversals over time.

fit together (Fig 5-4). About 200 million years ago, there was one supercontinent on earth, termed "Pangaea." This massive landmass later broke up into what eventually have become the continents of today. Numerous lines of evidence support the existence of Pangaea. Plant and animal fossils in geological strata older than 200 million years are similar on both sides of the Atlantic, indicating there was no barrier at one time. But after the continents split and were separated by this ocean, the fossil record reveals that living organisms evolved on each side in different directions, resulting in Old World and New World creatures. In addition, continental drift tore mountain ranges apart. Similar geological features between the Appalachians on the American east coast and mountains on the coasts of northwest Africa and western Europe demonstrate that these ranges were at one time joined together.

The most striking evidence for continental drift and the break up of Pangaea is the Mid-Atlantic Ridge. As the continental plates separated, molten rock from under the plates surfaced and then hardened, filling the growing gap (Fig 5-5). Some minerals incorporated radiometric materials when they crystallized, allowing the seafloor to be dated. Other minerals

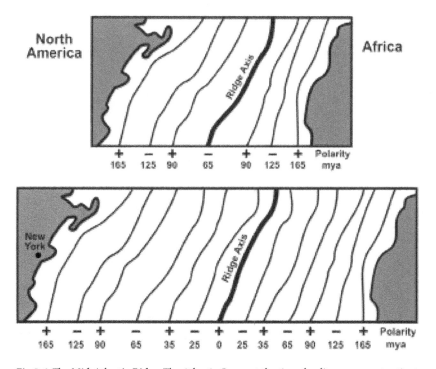

Fig 5-6. The Mid-Atlantic Ridge. The Atlantic Ocean at the time the dinosaurs went extinct was narrower (top) than it is today (bottom). As continents spread apart and pull their respective sea floor, molten rock from the core of the earth rises and hardens at the ridge axis. This diagram presents some magnetic stripes and their ages, indicating the time when they were at the ridge axis. mya: millions of years ago

incorporated iron and were oriented to the magnetic field of the earth as they cooled. This is similar to a magnet aligning iron filings. Consequently, stripes of "normal" polarity (as we experience today with the north magnetic pole in the north) are adjacent to stripes of "reversed" polarity (when the south magnetic pole is in the north). This indicates that the magnetic field of the earth has completely reversed many times. As a result, the floor of the Atlantic Ocean features a striped and mirror image pattern. Bands appear on either side of the ridge with the same date and same magnetic orientation (Fig 5-6). This geological data demonstrates that the Mid-Atlantic Ridge was not created in only a few thousand years.

To summarize, modern science clearly indicates that the earth is exceedingly old. The geological facts presented in this section are just a drop in the ocean of evidence. Many other dating methods exist, and like completely different and independent clocks, they date the earth well over

6,000 years. Of course, some Christians argue that God created the world with the appearance of age. But this strikes hard against the character of the Creator, implying deception. Such an argument also questions our divinely given ability to discover His world. I doubt that the Lord would have blessed us with the gift of a mind, only to have it lead us away from the truth and Him, since all truth is God's truth.

TRANSITIONAL FOSSILS AND OTHER EVIDENCE

When I became a born-again Christian and returned to church some thirty years ago, it was not long before well-meaning believers informed me that there was no evidence in the geological record for evolution. Their strongest argument was that transitional fossils did not exist. These are extinct creatures that are halfway in between the major classes of organisms like fish, amphibians, reptiles, and mammals. I was told that micro-evolution had taken place. For example, dogs had modified into different varieties, yet they still remained dogs. But people in my church stated with brimming confidence that macro-evolution had never occurred. They argued that there was no fossil evidence that fish had changed into amphibians, amphibians into reptiles, or reptiles into mammals.

This section challenges the popular belief held by many Christians today that transitional fossils do not exist. If evolution is true, then there should be fossils showing characteristics from adjacent classes of organisms, like fish with fins that are similar to the limbs of amphibians. In addition, these transitional fossils should appear in the geological record immediately before the appearance of a newly evolved class of animal, such as fish with limb-like fins just prior to the first amphibians. This section also introduces a few of the natural processes that account for these transitional features. The scientific discipline of evolutionary developmental biology, or "evo-devo" for short, is discovering that living organisms are quite flexible and that small changes in genes can result in large changes in anatomical structures. Again, by presenting this scientific data, I will only be scratching the surface. My purpose is simply to encourage readers to examine further this extensive body of evidence in the Book of God's Works.

Fish to Amphibians

Amphibians evolved from lobe-finned fish between 400 and 350 million years ago. In contrast to numerous thin splints of bone in the flat fins of ray-

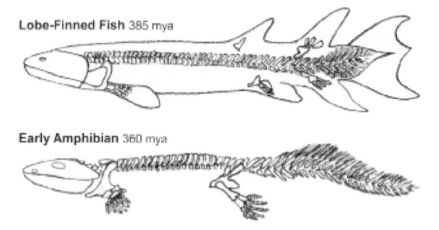

Fig 5-7. Lobe-Finned Fish and Early Amphibian. In contrast to the commonly seen 5 digits of most land animals, the limb of this ancient amphibian had 8 digits. See Fig 5-9 for an enlarged view of the anterior limb. Top: *Eusthenopteron*; bottom: *Acanthostega*. mya: millions of years ago. Redrawn by Andrea Dmytrash.

finned fish (e.g., perch, trout), lobe-fins are fleshy and have large, distinctly-defined bones. Many lobe-finned fish had both gills and lungs (modern lung fish are evolutionary descendants of these fish). This allowed them to survive in shallow, swampy, and plant-filled waters, as well as in regions susceptible to droughts. Their limb-like fins gave them greater mobility, and eventually allowed them to invade land and to find new sources of food. The first footprints of a four-legged animal in the geological record are of an amphibian that lived about 375 million years ago.

The fossil record presents many similarities between lobe-finned fish and the first amphibians. The body outline of the latter clearly mirrors the former—one of the earliest amphibians looks like a fish with legs (Fig 5-7). These two creatures also share a very rare dental feature. As Fig 5-8 reveals, they have labrinthodont teeth (Greek *laburinthos*: a maze; *odontos*: tooth). But the most remarkable transitional fossil evidence comes from the fins and limbs (Fig 5-9). Some lobe-fins evolved finger-like bones. Notably, there are 8 bones in the fins of a lobe-finned fish known as "the fish with fingers." It is no coincidence that the first amphibians often had 7–8 digits, pointing back to their origin from "fingered" fish. About 300 million years ago, these bones were reduced to the 5 digits commonly seen today in four-legged animals and us.

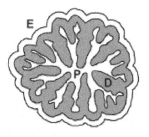

Fig 5-8. Labyrinthodont Tooth. Teeth are made up of an outside layer of enamel that covers an inner core of dentine. In nearly all toothed animals, the pulp canal is smooth and tubular, containing nerves, blood vessels, and other soft tissues. In contrast, lobe-finned fishes and early amphibians feature labyrinthodont teeth with a maze-like pulp canal. Fig 5-13 illustrates how these dental tissues develop. (E) enamel (D) dentine (P) pulp canal. mya: millions of years ago. Drawn by Braden Barr.

At the beginning of my biology PhD in 1991, I started to see a *pattern* with fossils that pointed toward the evolution of life, such as the transitional evidence between fish and amphibians. However, I was aware that scientists since the 1970s were admitting that the fossil record did not reveal the gradual change in organisms that Darwin had predicted. Leading the way, Stephen Jay Gould and Niles Eldredge proposed the theory of punctuated equilibrium. They argued that organisms remain the same for long periods of time (equilibrium) and then change rapidly in short bursts (punctuated). Of course, anti-evolutionists like me were quick to use this evidence against evolution. We argued that too many genetic changes, all occurring at the same time, would be required to account for the non-gradualistic pattern in the fossils. The chance of this happening through natural processes was highly improbable, if not impossible. However, our argument assumed a pre-1950s understanding of genetics in which one gene was responsible for one trait. Needless to say, we were quite out of date.

Midway through this doctoral program, I discovered *processes* in embryological development that could account for quick and dramatic evolutionary changes. In the newly emerging field of evolutionary developmental biology, experimental studies revealed that manipulating only one developmental gene or molecule could cause significant changes in the anatomy of an organism. This was the key notion that led me to accept evolution. Let me give an example. The fins of fish and limbs of amphibians, reptiles, birds, and mammals begin as buds at the side of the body. As these grow, similar developmental genes and molecules appear sequentially, but they are expressed in differing combinations between animals,

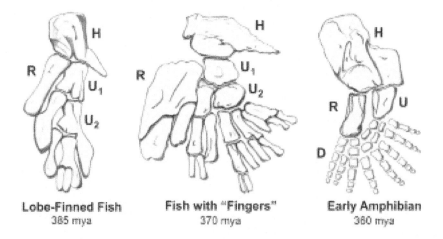

Lobe-Finned Fish
385 mya

Fish with "Fingers"
370 mya

Early Amphibian
360 mya

Fig 5-9. **Fin to Limb Evolution.** The pectoral (anterior) fin/limb of the "fish with fingers" is clearly a transitional stage between a pectoral lobe-fin and a front leg. It features the numerous arm bones of the former and the multiple digits of the latter. See Fig 5-7 for the body outline of the lobe-finned fish and the early amphibian. Top: *Eusthenopteron*; middle: *Sauripterus*; bottom: *Acanthostega*. (H) humerus (R) radius (U) ulna (D) digits. mya: millions of years ago. Redrawn by Andrea Dmytrash.

and this leads to different types of fin/limb anatomy. Simple experiments placing these molecules in a developing bud can alter the final number of bones in a limb and change their shapes dramatically (Fig 5-10).[3] Therefore, a minor genetic modification in the release of just one developmental molecule can produce different concentrations and combinations of these molecules, resulting in a major anatomical change. With this process in mind, and considering the fossil record of lobe-finned fish and the first amphibians, it was easy for me to see how fins evolved into limbs (Fig 5-9).

It is important to add that when I was a PhD student in biology, the fish with fingers had not yet been discovered. This was indeed a gap in the fossil record. But after my training, this fish and others with transitional fin/limbs were found, filling this hole in the scientific evidence. And they appear in the geological strata as predicted by evolutionary theory. In my opinion, this is the most amazing and powerful aspect of biological evolution. As new evidence is discovered, it always fits the basic theory.

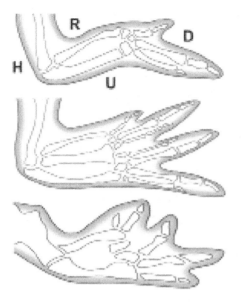

Fig 5-10. **Experimental Limbs.** The manipulation of genes and molecular processes in the developing upper limb of the chick can produce striking differences from normal bone anatomy (top). In one experiment, a limb appeared with 7 chick-like digits and a new bone between the humerus and radius (middle). Another experiment produced a limb with 5 digits similar in number to most land animals today (bottom). (H) humerus (R) radius (U) ulna (D) digits. Drawn by Kenneth Kully.

Reptiles to Mammals

The fossil record for the evolution of reptiles to mammals is quite complete and so gradual that their classification is difficult. In fact, the category of "mammal-like reptiles" emerged because scientists had trouble determining whether or not these animals were reptiles or mammals. In other words, they are clearly transitional creatures. The most distinguishing features in this evolutionary series appear in the teeth and jaws. As cold-blooded reptiles evolved into warm-blooded mammals, nutritional requirements increased. Therefore, a more proficient way to chew and draw nutrients arose in these animals.

The evolution of teeth from reptiles to mammals passed through numerous transitional stages. Fig 5-11 offers a few examples. Most reptiles have homodont teeth (Greek *homoios*: same; *odontos*: tooth). These are simple, cone-shaped, single-rooted teeth that are all about the same size and which are continuously replaced throughout life. They function well to grasp and kill animals, but are not useful for chewing. Consequently, reptiles swallow their prey whole or at least large parts of it, and they do not draw on all the possible nutrients of well-masticated food. As reptiles evolved into mammals, teeth began to lengthen at the corners of the mouth. This created a specialized puncturing weapon (the canine) and made these organisms more proficient killers. It also provided a tooth

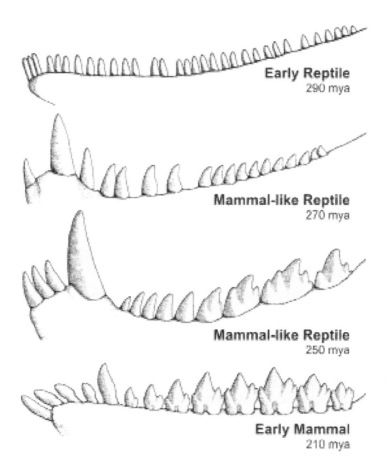

Fig 5-11. Reptile to Mammal Dental Evolution. See text for explanation. The double roots of the molars are evident in the early mammal. From top to bottom: *Protorothyris, Dimetrodon, Cynognathus, Morganucodon.* mya: millions of years ago. Redrawn by Braden Barr.

that could tear up the flesh of their victims. Later mammal-like reptiles featured a reduction in the number of cheek teeth and the beginning of cusps (the points on teeth), resulting in a dentition that could slice tissue. Finally, mammals arose with distinct incisors, canines, premolars, and molars. They also developed only two sets of teeth during their lifetime— baby and adult dentitions. The back teeth were multi-rooted, wider from front-to-back, and had cusps that interlocked with those of the opposing jaw. This last dental feature increased the proficiency of chewing and allowed mammals to extract more nutrients from their prey.

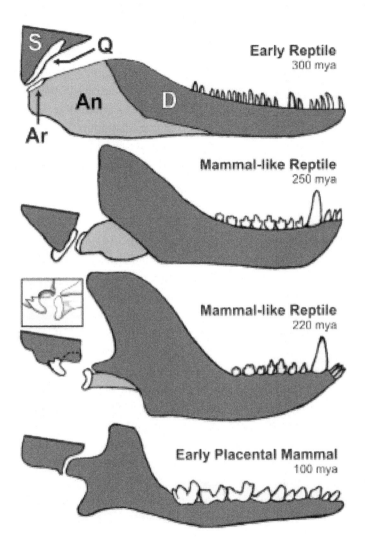

Fig 5-12. Reptile to Mammal Jaw Evolution. The inset shows an internal view of the double jaw joint in the second mammal-like reptile. A newly developed joint surface appears on the squamosal bone. Notably, the horizontal extension on the dentary bone associated with the joint in the early placental mammal eventually moves upward and is vertical in pre-humans and humans (see Fig 6-9). From top to bottom: *Haptodus, Thrinaxodon, Probainognathus, Daulestes.* (An) angular (Ar) articular (D) dentary (Q) quadrate (S) squamosal. mya: millions of years ago. Redrawn by Andrea Dmytrash.

The reptile to mammal fossil record also reveals different stages in the evolution of jaws (Fig 5-12). Reptiles have a lower jaw made up of numerous bones, and the jaw joint connects the articular and quadrate bones. In contrast, the bottom jaw in mammals is only one bone, and the joint is between two entirely different bones, the dentary and squamosal. As the reptilian jaw evolved, the dentary bone increased in size and the other bones reduced. Most remarkably, some mammal-like reptiles had two jaw joints—a reptilian joint and a mammalian joint. These are clearly transitional fossils, since they feature distinct characteristics from both classes of animal. Eventually, the dentary bone became the lower jaw in mammals, and the articular and quadrate bones separated from the jaws and reduced even further in size to become tiny ear bones (the incus and malleus, respectively).

A pattern definitely exists in the fossil record with regard to tooth and jaw evolution from reptiles to mammals, and evolutionary developmental biology offers insights into how these transitions occurred. In dental development, there is an incredibly complex series of molecular interactions between the tissues that produce the two basic components of a tooth—enamel and dentine (Fig 5-13). Different types of teeth feature different combinations of embryological molecules during development. Experiments reveal that the placement of specific developmental molecules in the front of the mouth can change the expected simple incisor tooth into a complex multi-cusped molar.[4] In other words, small genetic changes in the production and release of embryological molecules can easily produce the many different types of teeth seen in the fossil record.

Similar developmental mechanisms can lead to dramatic changes in the shape and number of bones in the lower jaw. As noted earlier, experimental limbs reveal that bone structure is very flexible (Fig 5-10). Evo-devo can also explain the appearance of a new joint in mammal-like reptiles. Basic embryological programs, like the instructions for teeth, are made up of groups of genes that are arranged in a sequence. These can be turned on or off at different times during development, and they can even be initiated at different places in a developing organism. For example, scientists have caused eyes to develop on legs and wings.[5] Thus, it would take only a small genetic change to switch on or turn off the gene program for a joint between two adjacent jaw bones, as seen in the origin of the mammalian jaw joint.

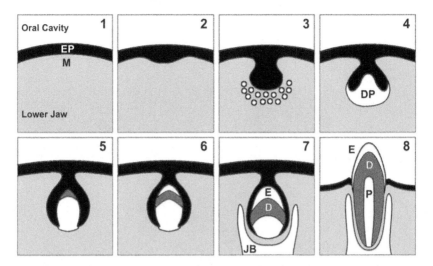

Fig 5-13. Tooth Development Stages. Incredibly complex molecular interactions occur in the jaw between the epithelium and the mesenchyme during the development of a tooth. The former tissue produces the outer layer of enamel, and the latter the inner core of dentine. Stages include: (1) prior to tooth development, (2) dental initiation and thickening of the epithelium, (3) bud stage with the early formation of the dental papilla which derives from mesenchyme, (4) bell stage with a defined dental papilla, (5) beginning of dentine production secreted from the dental papilla, (6) start of the epithelium laying down enamel on dentine, (7) crown stage with the development of the surrounding jaw bone, and (8) erupted tooth with a pulp canal, and the attachment of the tooth to the jaw bone. (EP) epithelium (M) mesenchyme (E) enamel (D) dentine (DP) dental papilla (JB) jaw bone (P) pulp. Drawn by Kenneth Kully.

Dinosaurs to Birds

During the last ten years, an explosion of fossil discoveries in China has supported the theory that birds evolved from small, two-legged, meat-eating dinosaurs. Nearly a dozen different species of these reptiles feature feathers, including down (fluff) feathers and flight (vane) feathers. Chemical analysis reveals that the feathers are made of the same basic protein (keratin) found in reptilian scales and mammalian hair. However, feathered dinosaurs did not fly. Down feathers first evolved for insulation and temperature regulation, allowing these reptiles to become more active. Flight feathers then appeared on their arms and tails (Fig 5-14). By flapping vigorously, this innovation allowed for "wing" assisted running and jumping, similar to a partridge today. It also permitted feathered dinosaurs to parachute and glide from trees. Eventually, these feathers increased in length and number, and flying birds appeared.

Fig 5-14. Feathered Dinosaur. Named *Caudipteryx* (Latin *cauda*: tail; Greek *pteron*: wing), this dinosaur had vane feathers on the arms and tail, and down feathers covered the body. Reprinted with permission.

The earliest birds feature a number of reptilian characteristics that indicate they evolved from dinosaurs. First, they have homodont teeth that are continually replaced throughout life (Fig 5-15). In contrast, birds today do not have teeth. Second, the first birds had long tails similar to those of reptiles. Modern birds lost this characteristic and have short tails. Third, three claws appear on each wing of the most primitive birds. These are almost identical to those on the upper limbs of small, two-legged, meat-eating dinosaurs. Claws are rarely found on the wings of birds nowadays. Finally, the first birds to evolve had a three-part lower limb similar to dinosaurs. It included a femur, a tibia and fibula, and elongated upright foot bones. As a result, birds and dinosaurs walked on their toes. The three-part leg remains in modern birds, but the upright foot bones have fused into one bone. In light of this evidence, it is clear that the first birds are transitional creatures between dinosaurs and birds today.

Modern birds also have vestiges indicative of their evolutionary past. For example, the small thin splint of bone that everyone finds when

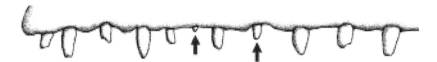

Fig 5-15. Teeth and Upper Jaw of the Famed Ancient Bird *Archaeopteryx*. Discovered in 1861, *Archaeopteryx* (Greek *archē:*) ancient; *pteron:* wing) became a celebrated transitional fossil supporting Charles Darwin's theory of evolution in *On the Origin of Species* (1859). Arrows point to replacement teeth that are in the process of erupting into the mouth. This dental feature and simple conical teeth are commonly found in reptiles (see Figs 5-11 and 5-12, top diagrams). Redrawn by Braden Barr.

eating a turkey or chicken leg is a remnant of the fibula. It was originally the length of the tibia as seen in reptiles, feathered dinosaurs, and the first birds (Fig 5-16). Similarly, during embryological development, the lower third of the leg in modern birds begins as three distinct units before these fuse into one bone. This developmental phase points back to the evolutionary ancestors of birds that had several separate bones in this part of the leg.

Dental features in birds today are another evolutionary vestige. As noted above, birds do not have teeth. The saying "as rare as hen's teeth"

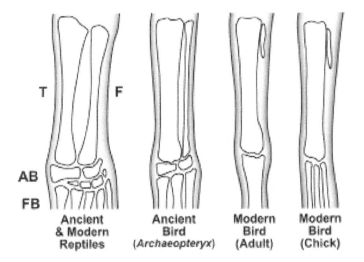

Fig 5-16. Lower Leg Evolution and Development. The ancient bird *Archaeopteryx* had fibula like a reptile. Similar to the reduction of bones in both the lobe fins of ancient fish (Fig 5-9) and the lower jaws of early reptiles (Fig 5-12), the ankle bones in birds also decreased during evolution. (F) fibula (T) tibia (AB) ankle bones (FB) foot bones. Redrawn by Kenneth Kully.

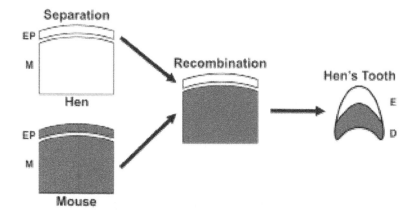

Fig 5-17. Hen's Tooth Experiment. Early in embryological development, scientists cut small pieces of tissue from the mouths of a mouse and hen. They placed the dissections in a solution with an enzyme that splits the oral epithelium from the jaw mesenchyme. The separated tissues were then put together in different combinations, and grafted into the animals to develop. The recombination in the diagram demonstrates that the mesenchyme from a toothed animal (mouse) can activate a dormant enamel gene in the epithelium of an animal that does not have teeth (hen). Since enamel is only produced by epithelium (see Fig 5-13), the enamel in this experiment was derived from the hen tissue, indicating its evolutionary history of descent from a toothed animal. (EP) epithelium (M) mesenchyme (E) enamel (D) dentine. Drawn by Kenneth Kully.

reflects this notion. However, a certain genetic mutation in chickens results in the development of rudimentary teeth.[6] But where did the genes to form teeth come from? The fossil record reveals that the first birds had teeth (Fig 5-15), and about 80 million years ago, they lost them. The reappearance of teeth in mutant chickens today indicates that though the genes for dental development were suppressed, they still remain intact. In fact, scientific evidence confirms that birds today pass through the earliest stage of tooth development. They express the same dental initiation genes and molecules found in toothed animals (Fig 5-13).[7] But this genetic dental program is cut short in modern birds and teeth never arise. Interestingly, scientists have discovered ways to re-awaken these dormant genes. Combining skin tissue from the mouth of a bird with the inner jaw tissue from a toothed animal causes the bird tissue to produce enamel (Fig 5-17).[8] Similarly, the placement of certain developmental molecules into the jaws of developing chicks can produce teeth.[9]

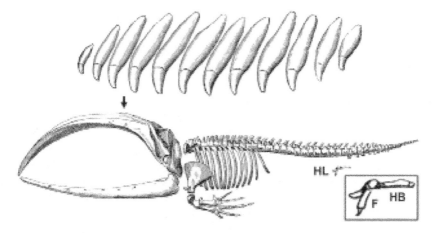

Fig 5-18. Modern Toothed and Non-Tooth Whales. Toothed whales have conical homodont teeth that often do not have enamel (top). In contrast to continuous tooth replacement and root resorption in reptiles, these whales have only one set of teeth (cf. Figs 4-7 and 5-15) with long, well-defined roots. Non-toothed whales have a comb-like array of plates, termed "the baleen" (not illustrated in the diagram), that attach to the upper jaw (bottom). These strain seawater and trap up to two tons of krill and small fish every day. Modern whales have a blowhole/s (arrow) on top of the head and only a small vestige of the hips and upper legs that is detached from the spine and "floats" in soft tissue of the tail (inset; cf. ancient whales in Fig 5-19). (F) femur (HB) hip bones (HL) hind limb. Top: killer whale (*Orca*); bottom: bowhead whale (*Mysticetus*).

Land Animals to Whales

Today there are two basic types of whales in the oceans; toothed whales like dolphins and killer whales, and non-toothed whales like massive blue and bowhead whales (Fig 5-18). It is important to note that whales are mammals, not fish. They have hair, are warm-blooded, and develop in the womb. They also have mammary glands and nourish their young with milk. Whales did not evolve from fish. Instead, they descended from land animals that entered the sea about 55 million years ago.

Readers will note that the title of this subsection does not refer to a specific ancestor from which whales evolved, but simply to land animals. This is because there is an on-going debate among evolutionary biologists. On the one hand, those who focus on the fossil evidence hold the traditional theory that mesonychids are the ancestors of whales. These are unusual mammals. They had a body similar to primitive herbivores (plant eaters), including hooves on their feet, and they had a skull with jaws and teeth like carnivores (flesh eaters). On the other hand, recent

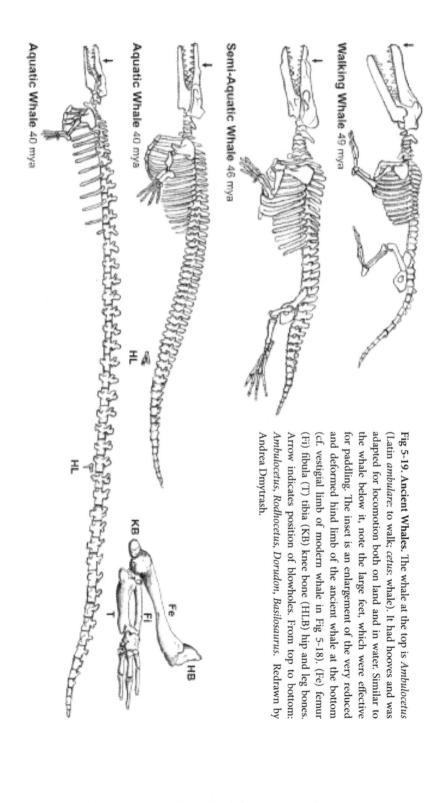

Walking Whale 49 mya

Semi-Aquatic Whale 46 mya

Aquatic Whale 40 mya

Aquatic Whale 40 mya

HL

HL

KB

Fe

T

Fi

HB

Fig 5-19. Ancient Whales. The whale at the top is *Ambulocetus* (Latin *ambulare*: to walk; *cetus*: whale). It had hooves and was adapted for locomotion both on land and in water. Similar to the whale below it, note the large feet, which were effective for paddling. The inset is an enlargement of the very reduced and deformed hind limb of the ancient whale at the bottom (cf. vestigial limb of modern whale in Fig 5-18). (Fe) femur (Fi) fibula (T) tibia (KB) knee bone (HLB) hip and leg bones. Arrow indicates position of blowholes. From top to bottom: *Ambulocetus, Rodhocetus, Dorudon, Basilosaurus*. Redrawn by Andrea Dmytrash.

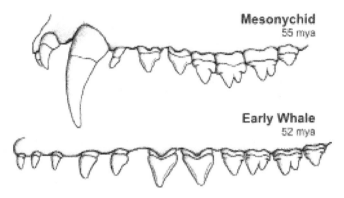

Fig 5-20. **Teeth and Upper Jaw of a Mesonychid and an Early Whale.** The anatomy of the molars is strikingly similar with both animals having double roots and similar cusps. The prominent canine of the mesonychid indicates a carnivorous diet, while the simple coned anterior teeth of the ancient whale is typical of modern whales (cf. killer whale in Fig 5-18). Top: *Sinonyx*; bottom: *Pakicetus*. Redrawn by Braden Barr.

genetic evidence indicates that whales and hippos are closely related, and those emphasizing this data reject the mesonychid theory. Though scientists disagree about which creature is the ancestor of whales, there is no debate whatsoever in the scientific community that whales evolved from land animals.

The fossil record for whale evolution features about two dozen transitional animals.[10] Fig 5-19 presents four examples. As whales evolved, the nostrils gradually moved from the front of the face to the top of the head where they became a single or pair of blowhole/s. Early whales had shortened limbs and enlarged feet, which allowed them to paddle effectively in the water. Notably, some still had hooves. Over time, the bodies of ancient whales became elongated and more streamlined for an aquatic environment. Their tails also enlarged and evolved into the main power source of locomotion through the water. Consequently, the back legs of primitive whales were reduced dramatically. Today, all that is left in whales of their hips and hind legs is a tiny, non-functional, boney vestige of their evolutionary past.

The first whales also featured molars that are strikingly similar to the land-dwelling mesonychids (Fig 5-20). These teeth had multiple roots and pointed cusps that were suited for slicing the flesh of prey. However, as these mammals began to live under water, chewing became very difficult and whales began to lose specialized teeth for mastication. In fact, the dentition of ancient whales is transitional. The teeth at the back of the jaw

Fig 5-21. Foetal Teeth of Modern Non-Toothed Whales. The crowns of the teeth are asymmetrical and irregular, and the roots are stunted and deformed. The open ended root indicates incomplete development (cf. stage 7 in Fig 5-13). Left and center: blue whale (*Musculus*); right: fin whale (*Physalus*). Redrawn by Braden Barr.

reflect their carnivorous past, while the front teeth are simple single cones like that of modern toothed whales (cf. toothed whale in Fig 5-18).

Finally, modern non-toothed whales feature an interesting vestige of their evolutionary history. As the fetus develops in the womb, teeth appear in the jaws (Fig 5-21). These never develop full roots, nor do they attach to the jaw bones. In fact, most of these malformed teeth are rejected from the jaws before birth or soon afterward. Being mammals, these whales are nourished through the umbilical cord in the womb, and they drink milk from their mother's mammary glands once born. As adults, they trap their food with the baleen and only consume small organisms (Fig 5-18). In other words, non-toothed whales have no need for teeth. But like modern birds, they still have tooth genes, which they inherited from their toothed evolutionary ancestors.

To summarize, the scientific evidence for biological evolution is powerful. Transitional fossils definitely exist. They appear in geological strata predicted by the theory of evolution. Evolutionary vestiges also exist. Remnants of anatomical structures are found throughout the fossil record and continue to be seen in living creatures today. Similarly, vestigial genes are present in modern organisms. In light of this evidence, some interesting questions arise for anti-evolutionists.

Why would God create a fish with 8 finger-like bones in its fins on the fifth day of creation, and then have it appear in the earth's crust between ancient fish and the first amphibians with their 7–8 fingers? Did He do this to test our faith in scientific concordism and a literal reading of Gen 1? And why would the Lord on this same creation day put tooth genes in modern birds and non-toothed whales? To give the false impression that life has an evolutionary history? No. I don't think so. Our Creator has gifted us with wonderful minds both to discover how He made the world and to glorify Him with scientific evidence, including evolutionary evidence. Of course, with the science presented above supporting the evolution of various living organisms, questions naturally arise in the mind of many Christians. Did humans also evolve? Is there any scientific evidence? If we did descend from ancient primates, what does this mean in regards to our bearing the Image of God and our being sinful? And what about passages in Scripture that state we all descended from Adam and that through him death entered the world? These are excellent questions that I will attempt to answer in the next chapter.

6

Human Evolution

THE CREATION OF HUMANITY is an explosive and divisive topic in the origins debate today. Most Christians fiercely defend that God created Adam and Eve as stated in the Bible. According to the survey mentioned in an earlier chapter, nearly 90% of born-again Christians in the United States believe that Gen 1 is "literally true, meaning it happened that way word-for-word."[1] The thought that we have evolved from pre-human ancestors is usually perceived as a threat to our dignity. For many, human evolution reduces us to "nothing but" animals controlled by physical impulses. To put it in popular language, the idea that we are related to extinct apes and have descended from them "creeps out" a lot of people.

Despite the volatility of human origins, four theological truths unite all Christians. First and foremost, God created humanity. We are not a mistake or merely an evolutionary by-product of blind chance. It was the Lord's plan to make people. Second, humans have been created in the Image of God. We are the only creatures that enjoy such a privileged status. This spiritual truth stands in sharp contrast to the atheistic belief that we are nothing but animals, and it commands us to respect both others and ourselves. Third, every man and woman is a sinner. We have all rebelled against our Creator, sinned against other humans, and even violated the creation. Everyone is responsible for their actions, and has control over their physical instincts and desires. On the Day of Judgment, God will call on us to give an account of our conduct. Finally, only Jesus offers redemption from sin. Acts 4:12 reveals that "salvation is found in no one else, for there is no other name under heaven given to men by which we must be saved." As far as I am concerned, these four theological truths are non-negotiable, inerrant Messages of Faith that are essential to Christianity.

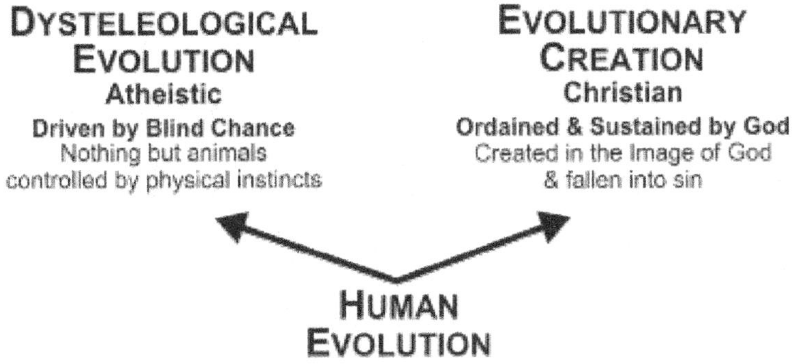

DYSTELEOLOGICAL
EVOLUTION
Atheistic
Driven by Blind Chance
Nothing but animals
controlled by physical instincts

EVOLUTIONARY
CREATION
Christian
Ordained & Sustained by God
Created in the Image of God
& fallen into sin

HUMAN
EVOLUTION

Fig 6-1. **Human Evolution: Two Interpretive Approaches.** This diagram reflects the Metaphysics-Physics Principle. The science of human evolution is based on observations and experiments from a wide range of disciplines, including geology, paleontology, genetics, and evolutionary biology. The ultimate belief in whether this natural process is teleological or dysteleological requires an intellectual-spiritual "jump" from this physical evidence to its metaphysical assessment.

Regrettably, the origins dichotomy has entrenched in the mind of most people the belief that God would never have created humans through evolution. This popular either/or approach also prevents many from entertaining the possibility that the Image of God and human sin could have been manifested during an evolutionary process that resulted in the creation of men and women. However, as we have already noted, the origins dichotomy is a false dichotomy. It not only inhibits Christians from seeing the scientific evidence for human evolution, but for non-Christians familiar with this data, it puts a stumbling block between them and an understanding of their true spiritual nature. To correct this situation, evolutionary creation offers a fresh approach to human origins. It asserts that physical evidence for human evolution is powerful, convincing, and indeed overwhelming. It also claims that God created humanity through a teleological natural process, which He ordained and sustained, resulting in marvelously designed creatures bearing His Image but fallen into sin. Fig 6-1 contrasts the evolutionary creationist view of human evolution against the atheistic interpretation assumed by many today both inside and outside the church.

This chapter presents a Christian approach to human evolution. It opens with some basic scientific evidence that indicates we evolved from pre-human ancestors. Next, three different models are presented to explore the manifestation of God's Image and humanity's sinfulness during the evolutionary process. The chapter closes with the sin-death problem. Genesis 3 clearly states that Adam's sin led to the beginning of physical death, and Paul repeats this notion in Rom 5 and 8 and 1 Cor 15. However, science demonstrates that death was in the world for 100s of millions of years prior to the appearance of humans. This is the greatest problem faced by evolutionary creation, and providing a reasonable solution to this conflict between the Book of God's Words and the Book of God's Works is absolutely necessary.

SCIENTIFIC EVIDENCE

Many Christians confidently claim that there is no scientific evidence to support human evolution. At best, they argue that the physical data is misinterpreted; at worst, they believe that it is fabricated and part of a secular conspiracy against Christianity. I once believed that the latter was the case. However, nearly all biologists today accept that human evolution is a fact of science. This section presents some basic evidence in order to encourage readers to examine further the scientific literature.[2] Like that in the previous chapter, this data hardly scratches the surface. But readers will see that there is both physical proof and a pattern that support the theory of our evolution from pre-human creatures.

One way to view human evolution is to compare it to a family. In both cases, living relatives share anatomical and genetic similarities. Resemblances are also seen between those alive today and those who are deceased. And like the genealogical tree of a family with different branches of related people, the evolutionary tree leading to humans has different pre-human species that are connected along ancestral lines.

Living Evolutionary Relatives: Anatomical Similarities

At every family reunion, physical resemblances are clearly evident. Similar noses, jaws, eyes, etc. often appear among relatives, even distant cousins. The similarities increase between individuals who are closely related, as seen with siblings and their parents. The nearest living evolutionary relatives of humans are the higher primates—monkeys, lesser apes (gibbons), and great apes (orangutans, gorillas, chimpanzees). Their basic anatomy clearly resembles ours, and the diagrams speak for themselves in Figs 6-2 to 6-4.

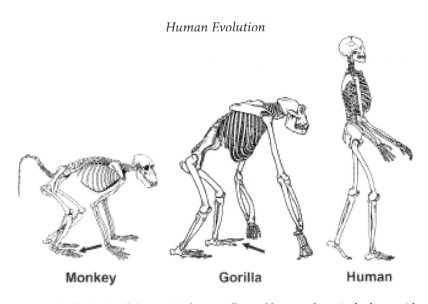

Monkey   **Gorilla**   **Human**

Fig 6-2. Similarities in Skeletons. Monkeys, gorillas, and humans share similar bones with differences in shapes and proportions. Skeletal anatomy reflects the type of locomotion on the ground. Monkeys are quadruped (walking on four equal-sized limbs), gorillas semi-quadruped (long-armed knuckle walkers), and humans biped (using only long-legged hind limbs). The big toe in monkeys and gorillas is angled away from the foot (arrow), allowing them to grasp and to move through the trees. Reprinted with permission.

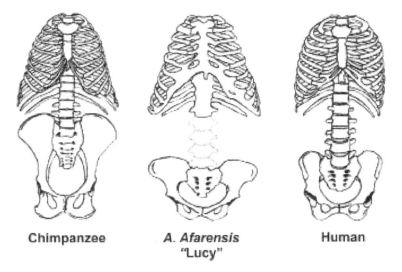

Chimpanzee   ***A. Afarensis***   **Human**
"Lucy"

Fig 6-3. Similarities in Rib Cages and Hip Bones. Chimpanzees have a pyramid-shaped rib cage. They also have massive hip bones that are characteristic of quadrupeds and semi-quadrupeds (see Fig 6-2). In humans, the former is more barrel-shaped and the latter shorten for bipedal locomotion. The pre-human *Australopithecus afarensis* combines some of these anatomical features. Commonly known as "Lucy," this creature had an ape-like rib cage and human-like hip bones. The latter feature indicates that she walked on her legs. Reprinted with permission.

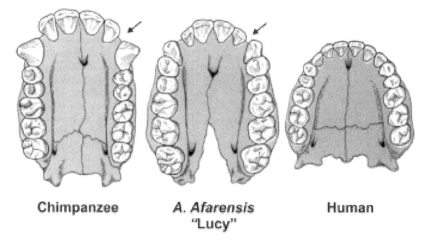

Chimpanzee   A. Afarensis   Human
"Lucy"

Fig 6-4. Similarities in Dentitions. Dental features in the upper jaw shared between chimpanzees and humans include: 6 square-shaped molars with 4 cusps (points on the tooth surface) at the back of the jaw, 4 pre-molars or bicuspids (2 cusps), 2 canines (eyeteeth) at the corner of the jaw, and 4 incisors in the front. Chimps differ from people in that the jaws and tooth rows at the back of the mouth are parallel to each other. Their canines are also very large and a space, termed the "diastema" (arrow), appears between it and the incisors. The posterior jaws and dental rows of humans curve gently and are angled toward the anterior, the canine is not prominent, and there is no space in front of it. The dentition of *Australopithecus afarensis* (Lucy) features the human characteristic of a small canine and the diastema found in monkeys and apes. The shape of this pre-human's jaws and tooth rows are slightly curved and between that of chimpanzees and humans. Reprinted with permission.

Living Evolutionary Relatives: Genetic Similarities

Genetic evidence demonstrates that humans are related to other higher primates. Just as the genes of immediate family members are more similar to one another than to those of distant relatives, science has discovered striking genetic similarities between our living evolutionary relatives and us.[3] Fig 6-5 reveals that monkeys are distantly related (93% similar genes), while chimpanzees are our closest "cousins" (99%).* It is necessary to emphasize that we did not descend from either of these primates. Regrettably, many Christians assume the theory of evolution asserts that humans evolved from monkeys or chimpanzees. Not true. We share ancestors that are now extinct. About 30 million years ago, the evolutionary line to monkeys separated from the branch leading to lesser apes, great apes, and humans. Around 6 million years ago, two distinct lineages descended

---

* More precisely, chimpanzees happen to be our 250,000[th] cousins because there are roughly 250,000 generations from the time we shared a common ancestor with them.

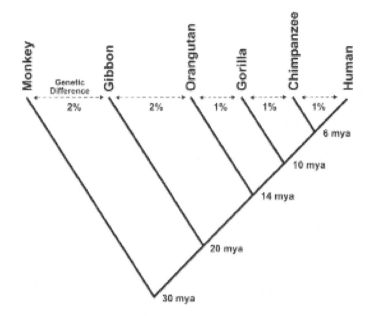

Fig 6-5. Humans and Higher Primates: Genetic and Evolutionary Relationships. Genes change very slowly over time at a relatively constant rate. This natural process is known as "genetic drift" and is caused mostly by random mutations in DNA. It functions like a "genetic clock" and estimates can be calculated for when evolutionary lines separated in the past. Notably, this genetic family tree aligns closely to the fossil evidence. mya: million years ago

from an extinct primate known as the "last common ancestor" (see Fig 6-8), and millions of years later, chimpanzees and humans evolved and appeared separately.

Evolutionary relationships between monkeys, apes, and people are also supported by the fact that they have similar defective genes, called "pseudogenes." Just like a bad trait that is passed down through a family (e.g., a genetic disease), genetic errors have descended along related evolutionary lines. For example, a gene required to produce vitamin C does not function in either chimpanzees or humans, and consequently a diet including this essential nutrient is needed for survival. Notably, it is functional in nearly all other animals. The existence of this same genetic error in chimps and people indicates that it was passed down from their last common ancestor about 6 million years ago (Figs 6-5 and 6-8).

Humans also have numerous olfactory (sense of smell) pseudogenes. About 600 of our 1,000 genes for the production of scent receptors are defective. In contrast, a larger portion of these are functional in lesser and

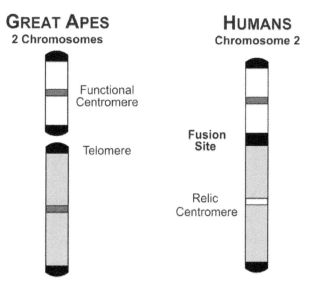

GREAT APES
2 Chromosomes

Functional
Centromere

Telomere

HUMANS
Chromosome 2

Fusion
Site

Relic
Centromere

Fig 6-6. Human Chromosome 2. Telomeres are present at the ends of every chromosome. A centromere is a region on a chromosome that connects chromosome pairs together during cell division. Human chromosome 2 features a telomeric region near the center and a nonfunctional centromere, indicating that this chromosome was originally two separate chromosomes similar to those found in chimpanzees, gorillas, and orangutans.

great apes, providing them with a keener sense of smell to detect food and enemies. But as the human brain evolved, new strategies emerged for nourishment and protection, thus reducing the need for a keen olfactory sense. In other words, there was no selective pressure by evolution to maintain this ability, and it was lost because genes naturally change over time. The fact that we have so many olfactory pseudogenes reflects our evolutionary history and relatedness to modern apes.

Finally, powerful evidence for human evolution appears in our chromosome 2. A genetic difference between the great apes and us is that they have 48 chromosomes (24 pairs), while we have 46 (23 pairs). As Fig 6-6 illustrates, the reason for this difference is that human chromosome 2 is made up of two previously independent chromosomes. A comparison of this chromosome with chimpanzee chromosomes 12 and 13 reveals essentially the same genes, arranged in a similar sequence along the chromosomes. In other words, after the evolutionary lineages leading to humans and chimps had separated from the last common ancestor (Figs 6-5 and 6-8), two chromosomes fused into one at some point along the evolutionary branch leading to our creation.

Deceased Evolutionary Relatives: Fossil Record Similarities

The pre-human fossil record offers some of the most tangible evidence for human evolution. It can be compared to the pictures in a family album. Anatomical similarities (shape of heads, jaws, teeth, etc.) appear between deceased relatives and living descendants. Family albums do not have photographs of every relative or of each moment in the life of an individual, yet no one doubts that generations of relatives have lived in the past and that they are connected to each other through ancestry. The fossil record is similar in that it offers "snap shots" of the descent from pre-humans to humans.

Fig 6-7 presents the facts for human evolution: the fossils and their dates.[4] The anatomical features between adjacent pre-human fossils are quite similar, and this makes classification difficult. For example, some scientists reject the genus *Paranthropus* and place the species *aethopicus*, *boisei*, and *robustus* with *Australopithecus*. As a consequence, it is not possible to determine with absolute certainty all evolutionary relationships and the pathway to humans. Nevertheless, this difficulty in classifying species indicates their relatedness, just like in a family. Fig 6-8 outlines one evolutionary tree based on the modern scientific literature. Though scientists debate over the interpretation of fossils and their relationships to each other, none question the fact that modern humans descended from ancient pre-humans.

Human evolution is supported by patterns in the fossil record that are both progressive and transitional. Regrettably, when I became a new Christian, there didn't seem to be anyone in my church that was aware of this evidence, or they simply did not want to deal with it for reasons I was unaware of (and which I'll mention later). But fossils exist that clearly show the evolution of skull anatomy and braincase volume over time (Fig 6-9). Evolutionary patterns are also evident in some notable pre-humans:

Australophithecus afarensis stood about 4 feet tall and is often described as being "ape from the waist up" and "human from the waist down." Best known from the famous fossil named "Lucy," this pre-human had a cranial capacity of 400–500 cubic centimeters, which is a little larger than a chimpanzee's (370–380 cc). *A. afarensis* walked upright on its legs and, as footprints from 3.5 million years ago reveal, in a fashion similar to us. Though the hip bones are comparable to ours (Figs 6-3), fossil evidence suggests that the feet had a long and angled first toe, indicating that

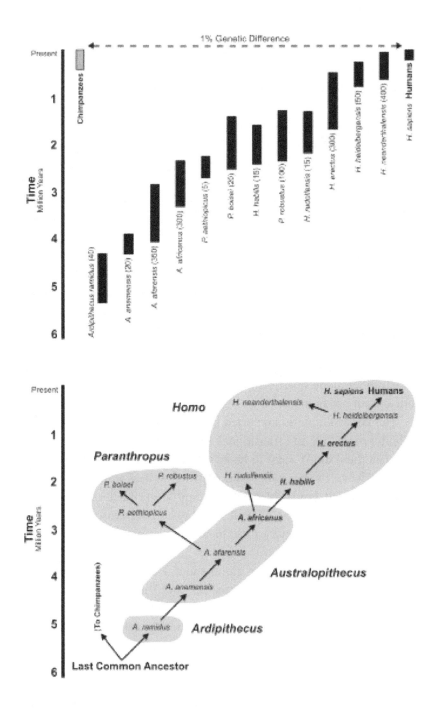

this creature could still grasp tree branches like a monkey or ape. Other transitional features appear in the jaws and teeth as seen in Fig 6-4.

Homo habilis was around 4.5 feet tall, had a brain volume of 500–750 cc, and hands that were freed from locomotion. Also called "handy man," this pre-human was the first species to make stone tools. These tools are found in archaeological sites dated at 2.5 million years ago, and they are next to animal bones that were cut and crushed. This evidence indicates that *H. habilis* severed flesh and extracted marrow from bone. The foot anatomy of this pre-human was remarkably similar to ours, suggesting that it walked proficiently but grasped poorly with its feet.

Homo erectus was proportionally similar to "humans from the neck down," stood about 5.5 feet tall, and had a brain volume nearing that of ours today. This was the first pre-human to leave Africa. Around 1.8 million years ago, it spread into the Middle East, and then Europe, South East Asia, and China. Archaeological evidence reveals that *H. erectus* developed sophisticated tools like spears and hand axes, controlled fire and cooked with it, and constructed primitive shelters.

Our species, *Homo sapiens*, is the last to appear in the fossil record. *Anatomically modern humans* emerged in South East Africa about 200,000 years ago. They moved into Mediterranean regions 100,000 years later. Their archaeological sites are not much different than those of the other pre-humans living at that time. However, around 50,000 years ago *behaviorally modern humans* arose in Africa. Archaeology reveals a dramatic change in the innovation and sophistication of their artifacts. This shift in behavior is often termed the "creative explosion" or "human revolution."

Fig 6-7. Pre-Human and Human Fossil Record (top). Evolutionary relationships are not presented in this diagram, only the period when a species lived. Pre-humans make up the evolutionary line to humans arising from the last common ancestor of humans and chimpanzees. The chimp is included for comparison. Since the genetic difference between us and chimpanzees is only 1%, it indicates that the genes of pre-humans differed even less. Consequently, debates are expected in classifying these species and determining their evolutionary relationships. The numbers in brackets roughly indicate the number of known fossil specimens. A: *Australopithecus*, P: *Paranthropus*, H: *Homo*.

Fig 6-8. Evolutionary Relationships between Pre-Humans and Humans (bottom). This diagram presents evolutionary pathways based on one interpretation of the fossil facts. Four genera (shaded areas) are outlined with their respective species. The skulls of the species in bold appear in Fig 6-9. *Ardipithecus* (Latin *ardi*: ground; *pithekos*: ape), *Australopithecus* (*australis*: southern; *pithekos*: ape), *Paranthropus* (*para*: near; *anthropos*: man), *Homo* (*hominis*: man).

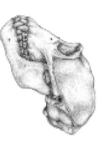

A. africanus
3.2–2.3 mya
430–515 cc

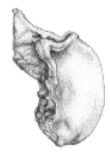

H. habilis
2.5–1.7 mya
500–750 cc

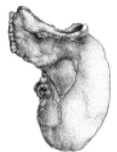

H. erectus
1.8–0.4 mya
700–1250 cc

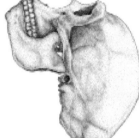
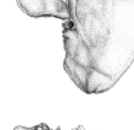

H. sapiens
0.2 mya to today
1200–1550 cc

Humans

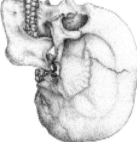

Chimpanzees
0.4 mya to today
370–380 cc

Fig 6-9. Evolution of Skulls in Pre-Humans and Humans. A number of features appear in skull evolution from *A. africanus* to humans. The face becomes flatter, the cheek and brow bones less prominent, and the brain case expands upward, downward, and backward. Note that the chimpanzee is not in this evolutionary lineage and it is included for comparison only. Skull volume in cubic centimeters (cc). Artwork © Copyright D. J. Maizels, 1994.

Current genetic research complements this archaeological evidence and demonstrates that there is little genetic variation among humans today. Consequently, all of us descended from a small population, estimated from 1,000 to 10,000 individuals, living no more than 50,000 years ago.

The scientific evidence for human evolution poses a number of challenging questions to both young earth creationists and progressive creationists. What is to be made of the fossil and archaeological records? They definitely show a progressive and transitional pattern indicative of physical and behavioral evolution: ape-like pre-humans ⇨ human-like pre-humans ⇨ anatomical humans ⇨ humans behaving like us. In particular, how are we to deal with transitional creatures like Lucy? She features both ape and human characteristics, and she appears in the fossil record (3.5 million years ago) about midway between us and the last common ancestor (6 mya) that we share with chimpanzees. Did God place her there to deceive us?

And what about the genetic evidence? If the Lord created humans *de novo* as stated in Gen 1 and 2, then it is puzzling why He would recycle two ape chromosomes and fuse them together to make our chromosome 2. As well, why would He put a functional gene for the production of vitamin C into most animals, but reuse the defective one He placed in chimpanzees for us? And what are we to make of the fact that 600 of our 1,000 genes for scent receptors are defective? Did God put them in Adam? All these questions are easily answered if the Father, Son, and Holy Spirit created men and women through an ordained, sustained, and design-reflecting evolutionary process.

THE IMAGE OF GOD AND HUMAN SIN

Most Christians claim that human evolution cannot be reconciled with the inerrant spiritual truths that we bear the Image of God and that we are sinners. Of course, the origins dichotomy and scientific concordism lie behind this assumption. These believers fail to recognize and respect the ancient science in Gen 1–3. They then conflate the existence of Adam with the Message of Faith that defines the two central spiritual characteristics of men and women. In contrast, evolutionary creation rejects scientific concordist interpretations of the biblical origins accounts, and separates the Divine Theology from the incidental ancient science regarding human origins. By embracing a complementary relationship between the Book of God's Words and the Book of God Works, this Christian view of

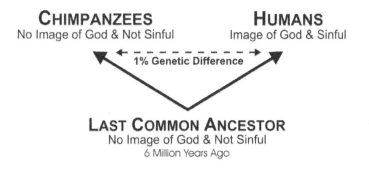

Fig 6-10. Evolution of Chimpanzees and Humans: Physical Features and Spiritual Realities. The Image of God and sinfulness are manifested only along the evolutionary line from the last common ancestor to humans. Note that the line in this diagram represents many branches like a tree and includes the numerous pre-humans found in the fossil record (see Figs 6-7 and 6-8).

origins offers a fresh perspective on the appearance of the Image of God and human sin during our evolution.

So Much More than Mere Flesh

Fig 6-10 outlines physical and spiritual relationships between humans, chimpanzees, and their last common ancestor. Science reveals that we share about 99% of our genes with chimps. In other words, the Lord has evolved a creature that *in the flesh* is nearly identical to us. But is there any doubt that we are radically different from chimpanzees? For example, has anyone read a novel or book of poetry written by a chimp? Where are their food banks, hospitals, and universities? Have they ever started a world war? Do they create environmental crises because of flagrant greed? Or how about chimpanzee religion? Where is their Holy Scripture? Do they sing praise and worship music? Is there a chimp messiah who died for sin? Are all of these behavioral differences between humans and chimpanzees accounted for by a 1% difference in genes? Hardly.

According to evolutionary creation, a radical shift occurred along the evolutionary line that eventually led to us and our extraordinary achievements and disgraceful transgressions. There is no evidence to indicate that this spiritual change happened either to the last common ancestor or along the chimpanzee branch of evolution. Evolutionary creationists assert that God created *only* humans "in His own image" and "likeness" (Gen 1:26–27). Men and women reflect aspects of the Creator's character, like spirituality, morality, and rationality. In particular, we enjoy the gift of boundless creative potential. Christian evolutionists also claim that humans are radically different from chimps and our common ancestor because we are the *only* sinful creatures in the world. People are capable of the most atrocious transgressions, like genocide and abortion. As the apostle Paul states, "All have sinned and fall short of the glory of God" (Rom 3:23). Therefore, instead of being a threat to Christianity, human evolutionary science complements the Bible in revealing that WE ARE SO MUCH MORE THAN MERE FLESH!!!

The Image of God and human sin are spiritual realities. Even though they are very real, they are not like physical entities or objects. Neither can be placed in a test tube to have its weight or volume measured, nor are they located in any particular organ or part of the human body. God's Image and human sinfulness are not like a virus that can be passed through a cough, a blood transfusion, or the touching of hands. Nor are they found in genes that are inherited from generation to generation. As spiritual realities, the Image of God and human sin are beyond and behind our physical reality. In other words, they are metaphysical realities (Greek *meta*: beyond, behind; *phusis*: nature, physical). At the same time, they are intimately related to our physical being, because it is through our bodies that we both reflect the Creator's likeness and break His commandments. Consequently, it is impossible to detect directly the Image of God and human sinfulness through scientific methods or instruments. Keeping this in mind, we can explore various approaches to the appearance of our unique metaphysical realities during our physical evolutionary process.

The Embryology-Evolution Analogy

Embryological development offers insight into the manifestation of human spiritual realities. We can ask some illuminating questions: While in our mother's womb, when do we begin to bear the Image of God? Do we get half an Image from her egg cell and the other half from our father's sperm cell? Or does our Maker inject divine likeness in a *punctiliar* (i.e., one precise point; Latin *punctum*: point) manner in development, such as at fertilization, the two-cell stage, after the first heartbeat, or at the start of brain activity? Or does God's Image originate in a gradual fashion across many embryological stages? Similarly, when do we become sinners? Do we get half a sin from the egg and the other half from the sperm? Or do humans become sinners at one specific moment in time like at fertilization, the two-cell stage, etc.? Or do we slowly become morally accountable

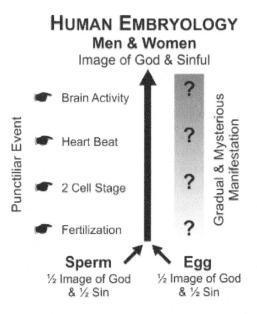

Fig 6-11. Origin of Human Spiritual Realities during Embryological Development. Many possibilities exist for conceptualizing the manifestation of the Image of God and human sin in our creation. The embryological stages presented are arbitrary and any other points/periods in development could be used. Compare with Fig 6-12.

and then sinful? Fig 6-11 summarizes this range of possibilities for the manifestation of human spiritual characteristics during embryological development.

Many Christians recognize that there are no clear and definitive answers to these questions. No biblical passage reveals when or how each of us begins to bear the Image of God during embryological development; or when or how we first fall into sin.[5] Nevertheless, these questions are informative. They thrust us to the edge of our human ability to know, and they force us to deal with the reality of mysteries. Our understanding is creaturely, and consequently, our knowledge is limited. As the apostle Paul recognizes, "We know in part . . . we see but a poor reflection" (1 Cor 13:9, 12). In fact, the Bible reveals that mysteries exist, and it employs this term over 30 times (e.g., Job 11:7; Dan 2:28; 1 Cor 13:2).

This is not to say that human knowledge has no value, because God created us with the ability to know Him and His world. Rather, it is to underline that our knowledge cannot penetrate all aspects of reality during this earthly existence. We will never grasp every facet of God's "ways and thoughts" (Isa 55:8–9). Therefore, I believe that the problems that arise in attempting to understand the appearance of the Image of God and sin during human embryological development lead to the conclusion that it is ultimately mysterious, and reflects God's ordained limits for human knowledge.

Recognizing this limitation in our creaturely ability to understand sheds light on the appearance of spiritual realities during human evolution. We can ask more instructive questions: When exactly did our pre-human ancestors begin to bear God's Image? Five million years ago? Three million years ago? With the use of the first stone tools? And how was divine likeness given to the precursors of humanity? Was it implanted in one punctiliar act in one single pre-human couple? Or did it come about through a gradual manifestation across numerous generations? Similarly, when did our non-human ancestors become morally responsible and fall into sin? Five million years ago, three million years ago, etc.? How did sin enter the world? Did it arise at one precise point because of one single act of rebellion against God? Or did humans slowly become accountable and sinful across many generations?

The Bible does not offer answers to these modern questions because the origin of humanity in Scripture is cast in an ancient science—the *de novo* creation of one man and woman. Yet this is not to say that the questions above are not good and fair questions. In fact, they must be asked because they bring us once more to the edge of our creaturely ability to know, and place before us another mystery. In the same way that we cannot fully understand the manifestation of the Image of God and sin in embryological development, I believe that the appearance of these spiritual realities during human evolution is just as mysterious.

Models of Spiritual Origins during Human Evolution

The origin of humanity is such a volatile topic in Christian circles today. In some churches and educational institutions, simply questioning whether or not we descend from Adam and Eve can lead to disciplinary action against a pastor, teacher, or professor. In fact, individuals like me have been barred from teaching in their denominational colleges and seminaries because we accept human evolution. Consequently, I believe that the best way to deal with this subject is to offer readers various approaches from which to choose.

Fig 6-12 outlines three basic models for the manifestation of both the Image of God and human sin during the evolutionary process. The parallels to embryological development in the womb are evident (Fig 6-11). It is important to note that the line between the last common ancestor and humans represents a large number of pre-human transitional creatures (see Figs 6-7 and 6-8). The three models include:

- *Evolutionary Monogenism* (Greek *monos*: one; *genesis*: beginning). This position suggests that God at one specific point in time selected a single pair of individuals from a population of evolving pre-humans.[6] He then intervened dramatically to implant His Image, and in an instant made them morally accountable. Soon afterwards, these two humans sinned through a specific rebellious act. The remaining pre-humans became extinct, and everyone today descends from this first couple, identified as Adam and Eve. As the epigraph at the front of this book reveals, Billy Graham is comfortable with this approach to human evolution.

- *Punctiliar Polygenism* (Greek *polus*: many). According to this perspective, the Creator at one point in time dramatically intervened to embed His Image into either all evolving pre-humans or a select group of these individuals, with the others going extinct. At that precise moment these beings were made morally responsible, but everyone soon sinned. This understanding of human origins suggests that there was one generation of many "Adams" and "Eves."

- *Gradual Polygenism*. This approach asserts that the Image of God and human sinfulness were gradually and mysteriously manifested across many generations of evolving ancestors. The origin of the spiritual characteristics that define and distinguish humanity is not marked by a single punctiliar event in the past. Rather, these metaphysical realities arose slowly and in a way that cannot be fully comprehended. The appearance of God's Image and human sin during our evolution is similar to the manifestation of these spiritual characteristics in our creation through embryological development: it is ultimately mysterious. Consequently, there was never an Adam/s or Eve/s.

Evolutionary creation embraces gradual polygenism. This approach to human spiritual origins is free from the assumption that the first chapters of the Bible feature scientific concordism. In contrast, evolutionary

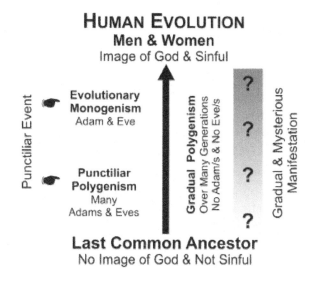

HUMAN EVOLUTION
Men & Women
Image of God & Sinful

Punctiliar Event

Evolutionary
Monogenism
Adam & Eve

**Punctiliar
Polygenism**
Many
Adams & Eves

Gradual Polygenism
Over Many Generations
No Adam/s & No Eve/s

? ? ? ?

Gradual & Mysterious
Manifestation

Last Common Ancestor
No Image of God & Not Sinful

Fig 6-12. **Origin of Human Spiritual Realities during Evolution.** The evolutionary line from the last common ancestor to humans in this diagram represents several branches like a tree and includes the many pre-humans found in the fossil record (see Figs 6-7 and 6-8). A number of possibilities exist for conceptualizing the manifestation of the Image of God and human sin during evolution. The placement of the three models on the evolutionary line is arbitrary and other points/periods could be used. Compare with Fig 6-11.

monogenism and punctiliar polygenism are concordist models, in varying degrees. Both appeal to punctiliar events in Gen 1–3: the quick and complete appearance of the Image of God in humans and the sudden fall of Adam and Eve into sin. However, the creation of humanity at one precise point in time, as recorded in Gen 1 and 2, is an ancient understanding of origins—*de novo* creation. And since the existence of Adam and Eve is ultimately dependent on this ancient science, then obviously their punctiliar creation in God's Image and their immediate fall into sin has no historical basis, because they never existed. *Evolutionary creation definitely accepts the manifestation of both the Image of God and human sin during evolution, but not through Adam and Eve.*

Evolutionary monogenism and punctiliar polygenism are proof text uses of Scripture. They tear the punctiliar events in Gen 1–3 out of their ancient scientific context, and then they conflate them with the current theory of human evolution. In other words, these concordist models mix ancient science and modern science. The problem with this interpretive method is the same as if NASA scientists used the 3-tier astronomy in Scripture to make calculations for launching rockets into outer space. Would any do that? Or stated another way, pinning an Adam and Eve, or Adams and Eves, to the tail end of evolution is like tacking the *de novo* creation of the firmament in Gen 1 on to Big Bang cosmology. Obviously, these are inappropriate uses of the Bible.

By respecting the limits and purpose of both the Book of God's Words and the Book of God's Works, evolutionary creation offers a complementary approach to understanding the origin of human spiritual uniqueness. This position acknowledges that humans evolved. But instead of threatening Christian faith, it is clear that somewhere along the evolutionary path to our creation a radical shift occurred that separated us from all other creatures—we became so much more than mere flesh. Evolutionary creation is free from the assumption of scientific concordism, and so it is not forced to envision the manifestation of the Image of God and human sin as punctiliar events in history. These spiritual realities arose gradually and mysteriously during human evolution. Despite our creaturely limits of understanding fully their entrance into the world, we know that we are the only creatures who have been made in the Creator's Image, we are the only creatures who have sinned, and we are all in need of a Savior.

THE SIN-DEATH PROBLEM

The greatest challenge for evolutionary creation is to explain biblical passages that refer to a connection between the sin of Adam and the origin of physical death. Genesis 3 indicates that death entered the world because God condemned Adam to die in judgment for his sin; Paul in Rom 5 and 1 Cor 15 understood the fall of the first man to be literal history; and the church throughout time has firmly upheld that this event in the garden of Eden is historical. However, the geological record reveals overwhelming proof that death existed for 100s of millions of years before the appearance of humans (Fig 4-3; page 84). Any Christian approach to evolution must deal directly with this problem and the sin-death passages in Scripture.

Biblical Passages

The opening chapters of Genesis clearly present a connection between human sin and physical death. God warned Adam, "You must not eat from the tree of knowledge of good and evil, for when you eat of it you will surely die" (2:17). But Eve gave Adam fruit from this tree, and "he ate it" (3:6). God then said to Adam, "Because you listened to your wife and ate from the tree about which I commanded you, 'You must not eat of it,' . . . you will return to the ground, since from it you were taken; for dust you are and to dust you will return" (3:17, 19). This condemnation came to pass, for "Adam lived 930 years, and then he died" (5:5).[7] It is necessary to underline that these passages deal with physical death, and not spiritual death, as progressive creation attempts to argue. The statement "for dust you are and to dust you will return" can only refer to bodily death.

The sin-death problem becomes quite acute in the New Testament. Romans 5:12–19 and 1 Cor 15:20–49 place Adam's sin and death along-side God's gifts of salvation and resurrection from the dead through Jesus. Paul states that "sin entered the world through one man, and death through sin, and in this way death came to all men, because all sinned. . . . For if the many died by the trespass of the one man, how much more did God's grace and gift that came by the grace of the One Man, Jesus Christ, overflow to the many!" (Rom 5:12, 15). This apostle also claims that "since death came through a man, the resurrection of the dead comes also through a Man. For as in Adam all die, so in Christ all will be made alive" (1 Cor 15:21).

The context of the latter chapter is quite significant. Paul is dealing with the question of Christians who have physically died, or "fallen asleep" (v. 6, 18, 20). He assures believers that "Christ has indeed been raised from the dead" (v. 20; also see 12–16, 35, 42, 52–53), and that God will also bring them back to life at the end of time (v. 23–24, 54–55). Clearly, 1 Cor 15 pertains to bodily death, and not spiritual death.*

There is also a connection between sin and death in Paul's conceptualization of the cosmic fall. Romans 8:20–22 points back to Gen 3:17–19 and God's condemnation of Adam: "Cursed is the ground because of you . . . for dust you are and to dust you will return." The apostle writes:

> For the creation was subjected to frustration, and not of its own choice, but by the will of the One who subjected it, in hope that the creation itself will be liberated from its bondage to decay and

---

* The term spiritual death is not found in the New Testament, but the notion is certainly present (John 5:24–25, 8:51; Rom 7:9–13, 8:6). Progressive creationists "spiritualize" the sin-death passages in an attempt to resolve the conflict between Scripture and the geological record, which they accept. They claim that Adam introduced spiritual death only. But as noted, Gen 3 clearly deals with physical death, and Rom 8:20–22 definitely presents a physical cosmic fall (see next paragraph). Therefore, forcing the idea of spiritual death into Gen 3, Rom 5, and 1 Cor 15 fails to respect the context of these passages.

brought into the glorious freedom of the children of God. We know that the *whole* creation has been groaning as in the pains of childbirth right up to the present time.

Romans 8:20–22 (my italics)

Note the context of this passage. Paul refers to the "whole creation," not simply to a limited region like the garden of Eden. By stating that "the creation was subjected to frustration," he indicates that there was a time when it was not in "bondage to decay" or "groaning as in the pains of childbirth." In other words, this apostle believed that the entire world was originally an idyllic creation. And this is clearly consistent with descriptions of the physical world in Gen 1 and 2.

In light of Gen 3, Rom 5 and 8, and 1 Cor 15, it is understandable why most Christians defend the cosmic fall and the connection between the sin of Adam and the origin of physical death. This is exactly what Scripture states. To strengthen their position further, these believers offer three arguments. First, they use a conferment argument. They contend that since Paul believed in the existence of Adam, then Adam must have been a real person. In other words, the apostle's belief in the reality of Adam confers historical reality to Adam. Second, these Christians employ a consistency argument. They argue that since Paul refers to Jesus as a historical person in Rom 5 and 1 Cor 15, then it is only consistent that his references to Adam in these chapters must also be to a real individual in history. Third, believers point out that the Gospel appears in these New Testament passages. In particular, it is explicitly stated in 1 Cor 15:1–7 and introduced by the clauses "the Gospel I preached to you, . . ." (v. 1) and "by this Gospel you are saved, . . ." (v. 2). They contend that we can't just pick-and-choose the Bible verses we want, such as accepting the Gospel and rejecting the existence of Adam. On the surface, these three arguments are quite reasonable. In fact, I used all of them when I was a young earth creationist.

But as noted in previous chapters, scientific predictions based on a scientific concordist reading of the Bible completely fail. If physical death entered the world because of Adam's sin, then the geological record should feature a pattern with human fossils at the very bottom, as depicted by either the young earth creationist prediction (Fig 4-5, page 88) or an old earth and cosmic fall prediction (Fig 6-13). However, the scientific facts reveal the appearance of humans at the very top of the geological column, 100s of millions of years after physical death had entered the world (Fig

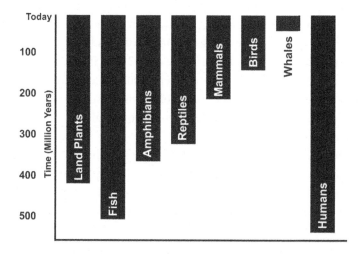

Fig 6-13. Old Earth and Cosmic Fall Fossil Pattern Prediction. This fossil pattern accepts both the geological record (with the exception of where science finds human fossils) and the biblical notion that human sin led to a physical (and not spiritual) cosmic fall.

4-3; page 84). This fossil pattern in the crust of the earth is as solid as the fact that we live on a planet that rotates on its axis and revolves around the sun.

It is important to note that a similar situation arose between Scripture and science during the 1600s. Galileo's astronomy challenged Christians to reconsider the meaning of biblical verses that state the earth is stationary and the sun moves across the sky daily (1 Chr 16:30; Pss 19:6, 104:5; Eccl 1:5). Today, none of us read these scriptures literally. Thus, we have a historical precedent to re-examine scriptures that present a connection between the sin of Adam and the origin of physical death. By focusing directly upon passages from the apostle Paul, let me propose four arguments that I have found helpful in moving beyond the sin-death problem.

Toward a Solution

First, let's reconsider the conferment argument. Many Christians argue that since Paul believed in the existence of Adam, then Adam must be a real person. But what else did Paul believe? In the wonderful Kenotic Hymn, he states that at the name of Jesus every knee should bow and every tongue confess that Jesus Christ is Lord in heaven, on earth, and in the underworld (Phil 2:10–11). Paul clearly accepted the 3-tier universe. But, does his belief confer reality to this understanding of the structure of the universe? And since he believed the world had three tiers, do we also have to believe it? More specifically, Paul accepted that there was a subterranean region where beings existed. Does his belief bestow reality to such a place under the surface of the earth? And if we decide to reject the 3-tier universe in Phil 2, but to accept Jesus as Lord, are we to be accused of being inconsistent? Or worse, of picking-and-choosing the Bible verses we want to believe? I doubt anyone would answer "yes" to any of these five questions.

Second, let me appeal to consistency in a way that is not often heard in churches. Consistency argues that since Paul accepted ancient astronomy and ancient geology, then he must also have accepted ancient biology. The static 3-tier universe was the science-of-the-day embraced by this apostle and his readers, and so too was the notion that living organisms were static and reproduced "according to their kinds." He refers to this idea in 1 Cor 15:39 by stating that "all flesh is not the same: men have one kind of flesh, animals have another [kind], birds another [kind], and fish another [kind]." Since Paul viewed living organisms as separately created kinds, it is only consistent that he understood the origin of life through the ancient biological notion of *de novo* creation. He presents this ancient science in Acts 17:26 in regards to human origins: "From one man God made every nation of men, that they should inhabit the whole earth." Paul definitely believed that human life began with the quick and complete creation of Adam. In other words, he accepted the biology-of-the-day.

Consistency also argues that since Paul had an ancient understanding of the origin of life, then he must have had an ancient view of the origin of death. For ancient peoples, death could only enter the world *after* the *de novo* creation of life. Or to state this in another way, a corollary (logical consequence) of quick and complete creation is that death can only happen *after* living creatures have been made (I will admit that this is a challenging idea to grasp. When I first heard of it, I had to think about it for a while). This ancient biological notion appears in Gen 3 and Rom 8 in conjunction with the lost idyllic age and cosmic fall. However, we know that living organisms were not created *de novo*, and consequently, death could not have entered the world as stated in the Bible. These are ancient scientific ideas with no correspondence to physical reality. Since this is the case, it is clear that the Holy Spirit's intention in Scripture was not to reveal how death actually entered the world. Fig 6-14 summarizes Paul's ancient science.

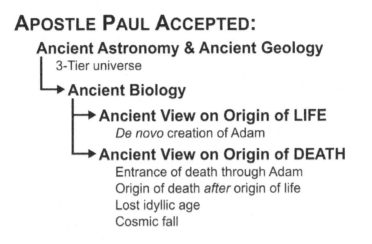

Fig 6-14. The Apostle Paul and Ancient Science. Paul lived in the first century AD, and like everyone around him, he accepted the science-of-the-day. As Phil 2:10–11 clearly reveals, this apostle embraced ancient astronomy and ancient geology. Consistency argues that he also accepted the biology-of-the-day, including the ancient notion that living organisms were created quickly and completely formed (*de novo* creation). And since Paul viewed the origin of life from an ancient phenomenological perspective, it stands to reason that he also had an ancient understanding of how physical death originated and entered into the world.

Third, common sense argues that the Holy Spirit used ancient science in revealing inerrant Messages of Faith to Paul and his generation. Of course, God could have disclosed scientific facts ahead of time, as assumed by scientific concordists. For example, it was well within His power to employ modern astronomy in Phil 2:10–11:

> At the name of Jesus every knee should bow—in God's celestial realm in another dimension, on every planet of every galaxy, and within the boundaries of the space-time continuum billions of light years wide—and every tongue confess that Christ is Lord.

But would Paul and his readers have had any idea of what was being revealed? Never. Just think of the Galileo affair less than 400 years ago. The issue was simply whether or not the earth moved, and Christians were quite troubled by that notion. As most know, the church even charged Galileo with heresy for believing that our planet spins on its axis.

To use another example, imagine if the Holy Spirit had employed modern evolutionary science and dictated to Paul word-for-word the following passage:

God created life through an ordained, sustained, and design-reflecting evolutionary process that included suffering and death over 100s of millions of years. During the evolution from pre-human ancestors to men and women, the Image of God and human sin were manifested gradually and mysteriously over many generations.

Considering the confusion and division that biological evolution produces in many churches today, would Paul or anyone in his generation have understood this passage? Absolutely not. This hypothetical divine revelation, like the one in the previous paragraph, would have been a disruptive stumbling block to faith. Instead, the Holy Spirit accommodated to the level of the apostle and his readers in the revelatory process by using the science-of-their-day, including an ancient biology regarding the origins of both life and death. In other words, God met them where they were.

Fourth, it is necessary to underline that Jesus and His sacrifice on the Cross are not dependent on the existence of Adam. Now, there is no doubt that Paul believed in the historical reality of both Adam and Jesus. In particular, this apostle recognized that the Gospel is based on the Lord's existence and His physical resurrection from the grave. Stating concisely the Good News and its implications, Paul writes:

> Now, brothers, I want to remind you of the Gospel I preached to you, which you received and on which you have taken your stand. By this Gospel you are saved, if you hold firmly to the word I preached to you. Otherwise you have believed in vain.
>
> For what I received I passed on to you as of first importance: that Christ died for our sins according to the Scriptures, that He was buried on the third day according to the Scriptures, and that He appeared to Peter, and then to the Twelve. After that, He appeared to more than five hundred of the brothers at the same time, most of whom are still living, though some have fallen asleep. Then He appeared to James, then to all the apostles, and last of all He appeared to me also, as to one abnormally born. . . .
>
> And if Christ has not been raised, our preaching is useless and so is your faith. . . . And if Christ has not been raised, your faith is futile; you are still in your sins.
>
> 1 Corinthians 15:1–7, 14, 17

Please Note: this is the Gospel as stated in the Bible, and there is no mention whatsoever of Adam and whether or not he existed. Christian faith is founded on Jesus, not Adam. Also note that this passage refers to many people who lived during a well-known point in real history (first century AD) and who had actually met the Lord.[8] This is not the case with Adam. Of course, Paul believed that Adam existed, and mentions him later in 1 Cor 15. But Adam's existence is based on *de novo* creation, the origins science-of-the-day for Paul and his readers. Therefore, in the same way that we must separate, and not conflate, the inerrant message that Jesus is Lord from the fact that the 3-tier world presented in Phil 2 does not exist; we must also separate, and not conflate, the historical reality of Jesus and His bodily resurrection from the fact that Adam never existed, because Adam's existence is rooted in an ancient biology of human origins.

This sheds new light on the popular consistency argument. Many Christians contend that since Paul refers to Jesus as a historical individual in Rom 5 and 1 Cor 15, then references to Adam in these chapters must also be to a real person in history. However, this common line of reasoning fails to distinguish real history (the existence of Jesus) from an ancient understanding of human origins (the *de novo* creation of Adam). In other words, the well-used consistency argument is in fact inconsistent! It conflates actual historical events of the first century AD with an ancient biology. This is similar to using Phil 2 and the historical fact that Jesus existed in order to argue for the existence of the 3-tier universe presented in that chapter; and then to extend the ancient astronomy in this New Testament passage back to Gen 1 to claim that God actually created a world with three tiers. I am doubtful that anyone would appeal to consistency in such a way.

Considering the four arguments above, it is possible to suggest a new approach to Rom 5 and 8 and 1 Cor 15. References to a connection between the sin of Adam and the origin of physical death should be interpreted using the Message-Incident Principle, as presented in Fig 6-15. The central message in these biblical chapters is this: we are sinners and God judges us for our sins, but the Good News is that He offers us the hope of eternal life through the sacrificial death of Jesus and His physical resurrection from the dead. In order to deliver as effectively as possible spiritual truths about human sinfulness and the divine judgment of sin, the Holy Spirit accommodated to Paul's level by employing incidental ancient biological notions from Gen 2–3: the *de novo* creation of Adam, the entrance of physical death into the world through Adam, the lost idyllic age, and the cosmic fall. To be sure, this is a very complex and counterintuitive way to read Scripture. Nevertheless, we must not conflate, but instead separate

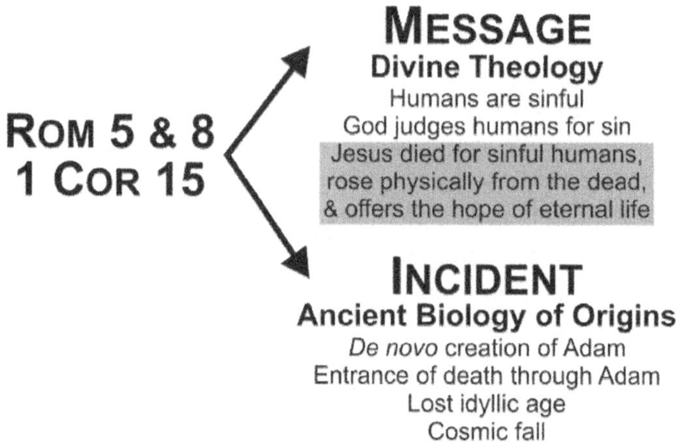

MESSAGE
Divine Theology
Humans are sinful
God judges humans for sin
Jesus died for sinful humans,
rose physically from the dead,
& offers the hope of eternal life

ROM 5 & 8
1 COR 15

INCIDENT
Ancient Biology of Origins
De novo creation of Adam
Entrance of death through Adam
Lost idyllic age
Cosmic fall

Fig 6-15. **Romans 5 and 8 and 1 Corinthians 15 & the Message-Incident Principle.** A solution to the sin-death problem suggests that we must separate the life-changing Messages of Faith in Scripture, including the Gospel of Jesus (shaded area), from the incidental ancient biological understanding of the origin of life and death.

the inerrant Messages of Faith from their incidental ancient vessel in Rom 5 and 8 and 1 Cor 15. These passages in the Word of God do not reveal *how* sin entered the world, but *that* we are sinners in need of a Savior, whom God has graciously sent to die on the Cross for us.

To conclude, there is no sin-death problem. Adam never existed, and consequently, sin did not enter the world through him. Nor then did physical death arise as a divine judgment for his transgression, because once again, Adam never existed. The origin of death presented in Gen 3 is rooted deeply in the ancient scientific notions of the lost idyllic age and cosmic fall. Therefore, human sin is not connected to physical death, and no conflict exists between Gen 3 and the fossil record. Indeed, sin did enter the world, but not through Adam.

7

Putting Origins in Perspective

M Y CENTRAL CONCLUSION IN this book is clear: God created the universe and life through evolution, and this fact has no impact whatsoever on the foundational beliefs of Christianity. Now I'm certainly aware of how shocking this statement is not only to most Christians, but also to non-Christians. And I fully expect to receive more than my fair share of criticism. Twenty-five years ago I would have been first in line to attack anyone holding my view of origins. So, do I get upset with critics who might be less than charitable? No, not at all. Actually, I very much respect and commend their passion for the faith. Yet I must point out to my brothers and sisters in Christ that the Jesus I knew and loved as a young earth creationist is the very same Jesus I know and love today as an evolutionary creationist. We serve the same Lord.

I must also underline that after becoming an evolutionist, my love for Jesus and the Bible hasn't changed one bit since the time I was a six-day creationist. I continue to feel His presence daily, especially when reading Scripture for my spiritual nourishment. My prayer life is the same, and the sense of calling to defend Christianity still burns in my soul. And my moral positions and yearning for holiness remain intact, though I am certainly not a perfect Christian. If anything has changed, my studies in evolutionary biology have led me to a greater appreciation for the reflection of intelligent design in nature. As well, my charismatic experiences with signs and wonders have increased. It was God's grace through faith that saved me from my sinfulness nearly thirty years ago, and it is the Lord's love that continues to infuse my life with meaning and comfort after coming to terms with evolution.

Over the last ten years, my academic research has focused on attempting to develop an approach to evolution that is faithful to Christianity.

During this period, I have presented evolutionary creation in a wide variety of secular and religious settings: universities, colleges, and seminaries; professional conferences for teachers, theologians, and scientists; the general public through lectures, debates, radio, and television programs; and some Roman Catholic and evangelical Protestant churches. In almost every case, the dialogue has been wonderfully respectful, and I have valued the questions and challenges that people have offered. Indeed, they have profoundly shaped my thinking. Of course, not everyone agrees with my view of origins, and I certainly do not expect them to. My primary goal is to stimulate discussion for the possibility that the God of the Bible created through an ordained, sustained, and design-reflecting evolutionary process, and for us to consider the implications. In particular, I want young people to be aware that evolutionary creation is a reasonable option. I do not for one moment believe that my view is *the* Christian position on evolution. It simply outlines *an* approach to this topic.

There is one response to my work that has impacted me over the years and led me to believe that I am at least headed in the right direction. It comes from evangelical Christians who have studied science, evolutionary biology in particular. Once introduced to the basic principles of evolutionary creation, they tell me that they have intuitively held this position in a loose and undefined way for quite a long time. Now equipped with this category, these believers enjoy firm ownership of their view of origins.

I have seen a similar response in my science-religion courses, especially from many of the pre-med students who are born-again Christians. In preparing for medical school, they see evolutionary evidence almost every day in their biology classes. But on Sunday at church, they are told to beware of evolution. A number of them have admitted that they entered my introductory course with their faith and science in disconnected compartments in their mind. This was the only way to make sense of the world and to have some sort of peace regarding origins. I'll never forget the best student in one of my first classes. She attended a fine evangelical church and was about to leave for medical school. Her parting words to me were, "I am now free." Yes, indeed. Free to enjoy the Book of God's Words and the Book of God's Works, and free to use these divine revelations to build a fully integrated Christian worldview.

Let's close with some final thoughts in hope of putting origins in perspective. To assist me, I'll use a number of questions that Christians have often asked me over the years about evolutionary creation. And we will end with the true story mentioned in the preface of this book. I'll attempt to answer the question a high school student asked a leading anti-evolutionist several years ago: "What about dinosaurs, how do they fit into the Bible?"

How Can Evolution Reflect Intelligent Design?

Many people today find it difficult, if not impossible, to see a relationship between evolution and intelligent design. The leaders of the Intelligent Design Movement (Intelligent Design Theory) are responsible for this situation.* They have thrust a large wedge between design and evolution, creating a dichotomy. However, this is another false dichotomy. Let me offer an analogy to explain an evolutionary creationist perspective on the biblical fact that nature reflects intelligence and the scientific fact that the universe and life evolved.

Imagine that God's creative action in the origin of the world is like the stroke of a cue stick in a game of billiards. Divide and label the balls into three groups using the words heavens, earth, and living organisms, and let the 8-ball represent humanity. The young earth creationist depicts the Creator making single shot after single shot with no miscues until all the balls are off the table. No doubt, that's remarkable. A progressive creationist sees the opening stroke that breaks the balls as the Big Bang. All of the balls labeled heavens and earth are sunk by this initial shot. Then God sinks those that signify living organisms and humans individually. That's even more impressive.

Evolutionary creationists claim that the God-of-the-individual-shots, like the God-of-the-gaps, fails to reveal fully the power and foresight of the Designer. According to this view of origins, the breaking stroke is so incredibly precise and finely tuned that not only are all the balls sunk, but they drop in order. It begins with those labeled heavens, then earth, followed by living organisms, and finally the 8-ball—the most important ball in billiards—representing humans. And to complete the analogy, the Lord pulls this last ball out of the pocket and holds it in His hands to show His personal involvement with men and women. Is such a God not infinitely more talented than that of the anti-evolutionists? Are His eternal power and divine nature not best illustrated in the last example? Doesn't

---

* See the footnote on pages 8–9.

the evolutionary creationist depiction of the Creator provide the most magnificent reflection of intelligent design?

This is how I see design in evolution. I certainly agree with young earth creationists and progressive creationists that the structure and operation of the present world points to a Designer. But evolutionary creationists have a greater and more complete view of design than the anti-evolutionists. We include the incalculable number of evolutionary processes in the origin of the universe and life, so the declaration of God's glory extends to the amazing self-assembling character of the creation. Yet despite differences between Christians on *how* intelligent design arose in the world, we must never forget that we stand united in affirming *that* nature clearly reflects the designing intelligence of our Creator.

And we all agree that every man and woman is accountable before the Lord with regard to this natural revelation inscribed deeply into the world. I will go so far as to make the following speculation: On the Day of Judgment, anyone who claims that there was no evidence for the existence of a Creator will be reminded of the countless times "the heavens declared the glory of God" (Ps 19:1) . . . and then they will be told that "they are without excuse" (Rom 1:20).

Why Did God Create through Evolution?

This question needs to be answered in three parts. First, let's put this in perspective: God can do whatever He wants. This may seem blunt, but after all, He is God. He could have made the world as understood by either young earth creation or progressive creation, since it is well within His power to do so. Obviously, it is the Creator's decision, no matter what assumptions or expectations we may have. If He created us through evolution, who are we to question His choice of creative method? As the apostle Paul asks, "But who are you, O man, to talk back to God? Shall what is formed say to Him who formed it, 'Why did you make me like this?'" (Rom 9:20).

Second, we must always remember that faith is foundational to our existence. The Bible clearly states that it is a requirement for our relationship with the Lord (Matt 17:20; John 20:29; Eph 2:8). In a wonderful chapter explaining the meaning of faith, the author of the book of Hebrews begins:

> Now faith is being sure of what we hope for and certain of what we
> do not see. This is what the ancients were commended for. By faith

> we understand that the universe was formed at God's command,
> so that what is seen was not made out of what was visible.

Hebrews 11:1–3

We might be "sure" and "certain" that God made the world, but ultimately, this assuredness is rooted in faith. As the Metaphysics-Physics Principle underlines, everyone makes a leap of faith (Fig 1-4; page 12). Therefore, all attempts at *proving* the existence of the Creator through science are not biblical. The problem with the anti-evolutionary positions is that they try to put God into a test tube in order to *prove* that He exists. If the geological record aligned with the scientific predictions of either young earth creation or progressive creation, then there would be no debate (Fig 4-5, page 88; Fig 4-8, page 91). This would be incontestable *proof* for the existence of the God of the Bible. Accepting the Lord would be limited to science and simple logic, nothing more. And if this were the case, faith would not be required "to understand that the universe was formed at God's command."

Finally, to answer the question in the title of this subsection directly, I believe that God created through evolution because an evolutionary world is the perfect stage upon which to develop a genuine relationship with Him. In stating that creation is perfect, I am not affirming the traditional belief in an original paradise. The notion of an idyllic age is ancient science with no correspondence to reality. Instead, this "very good" (Gen 1:31) evolved creation does not force us to believe in God, because it offers an environment within which we have real freedom to accept or reject Him. If anti-evolutionary fossil patterns existed, they would crush free choice. A young earth creation or progressive creation would be coercive and it would destroy human freedom. But an evolutionary creation allows men and women to view evolution as nothing but a dysteleological natural process, and to assume that no Creator exists. At the same time, in an evolved world we can see reflections of intelligent design pointing toward our Maker, and we have the freedom to pursue a personal relationship with Him. Both options are open to us.

The God of Love does not force Himself upon us, because that is not the nature of love. In the same way that you cannot coerce anyone into loving you, it is impossible for the Lord to make you love Him. An evolutionary creation is the ideal world in which to fall in love with God and to experience His unfathomable love for us. It is the perfect creation where we can truly and freely fulfill Jesus' commandment to "love the Lord your

God with all your heart and with all your soul and with all your mind" (Matt 22:37).

Why Did God Use Ancient Science in the Bible?

An important theme that I have repeated throughout this book is that God meets us wherever we happen to be. This is an amazing aspect of God's grace. Even in the depths of our sin and foolishness, He comes down to our level to reveal His profound love for us. Anyone who knows the Lord personally experiences this undeserved act of accommodation. In the same way, when the Holy Spirit inspired the biblical writers of the origins accounts, He employed their understanding of the physical world—an ancient science that featured a 3-tier universe in which living organisms, including humans, were created *de novo*. Of course, it was well within God's power to reveal modern science ahead of time. He could have dictated to the authors of the origins accounts that the Big Bang and biological evolution were His creative methods. But would anyone at that time have had any idea what these natural processes were? No. In fact, such a revelation would have been a stumbling block, distracting readers from the Messages of Faith. Scripture had to be accommodated in order to be understood by ancient peoples.

I certainly appreciate that my approach to the biblical accounts of origins troubles many Christians. They are quick to ask me: If Adam never existed and the events in Gen 1–3 did not actually happen, then is this also true with Jesus, His crucifixion, and bodily resurrection? The answer to this question lies in the foundational interpretive principle of literary genre. The early chapters of Scripture and the Gospels are completely different types of literature. So no, the interpretive method I present in this book for the biblical accounts of origins is *not* applicable to the New Testament and the record of the Lord's ministry. Genesis 1–3 is structured on ancient science—the *de novo* creation of the world and the lost idyllic age. In sharp contrast, the New Testament is based on the eyewitness testimony of real people who actually encountered Jesus.[1]

Let me offer three examples to support my case. Some eyewitnesses to the life of Jesus wrote down their experiences, like the apostle John. He opens his first letter:

> That which was from the beginning, which we have heard, which we have seen with our eyes, which we have looked at and our hands have touched—this we proclaim concerning the Word of Life. The

life appeared; we have seen it and testify to it, and we proclaim to you the eternal life, which was with the Father and has appeared to us. We proclaim to you what we have seen and heard, so that you also may have fellowship with us. And our fellowship is with the Father and with his Son, Jesus Christ.

1 John 1:1–3

John's intention of offering a historical account of the Lord also appears at the end of his gospel. He concludes, "This is the disciple who testifies to these things and who wrote them down. We know that his testimony is true. Jesus did many other things as well. If every one of them were written down, I suppose that even the whole world would not have room for the books that would be written" (John 21:24–25).

The apostle Peter was another eyewitness to the events surrounding Jesus. He made it very clear in his second letter that he was proclaiming real history, and not imaginary tales:

We did not follow cleverly invented stories when we told you about the power and coming of our Lord Jesus Christ, but we were eyewitnesses of his majesty. For he received honor and glory from God the Father when the voice came to him from the Majestic Glory, saying, "This is my Son, whom I love; with him I am well pleased." We ourselves heard this voice that came from heaven when we were with him on the sacred mountain.

2 Peter 1:16–18

In this passage, Peter is referring to the transfiguration of Jesus. This miracle was also seen by James and John, and recorded by gospel writers in Matt 17:1–8, Mark 9:2–8, and Luke 9:28–36. Clearly, the purpose of all these New Testament passages was to reveal that an actual event occurred in the past.

Finally, in outlining his writing method, Luke is strikingly similar to a modern historian. He begins his gospel:

Many have undertaken to draw up an account of the things that have been fulfilled among us, just as they were handed down to us by those who were eyewitnesses and servants of the Word. Therefore, since I myself have carefully investigated everything from the beginning, it seemed good also to me to write an orderly account for you, most excellent Theophilus, so that you may know with certainty of the things you have been taught.

Luke 1:1–4

Luke's intention is to present real history that was experienced by real people. His purpose is "to write an orderly account" of the actual events surrounding the ministry of Jesus in order that it "may be known with certainty." Like a historian today, his method is a "careful investigation" of "handed down" sources, which include those of "eyewitnesses." And most importantly, Luke interprets history as being "fulfilled" in his day by Jesus through the Incarnation and His sacrificial death on the Cross.

So, to repeat it word-for-word a second time: the interpretive method I present in this book for the biblical accounts of origins is *not* applicable to the New Testament and the record of the Lord's ministry. Genesis 1–3 and the New Testament writings are different types of literature and they require different interpretive approaches.

What never ceases to amaze me is that even though Christians in every generation have overlooked the ancient science in Gen 1–3, they have consistently identified the Messages of Faith. Church history reveals that those who are on their knees before the Word of God have always discerned the life-changing eternal truths, despite their skill level in biblical interpretation. As a new Christian with no appreciation of the ancient science in the biblical origins accounts, I was able to grasp that God was the Creator, the world was very good, we were created in His Image, we are all sinners, and He judges us for our sins. Even today, young earth creationists, progressive creationists, and evolutionary creationists all agree that these are the most important inerrant spiritual truths in Gen 1–3. Indeed, as the Lord states, "My Word goes out from my mouth; it will not return to Me empty, but will accomplish what I desire and achieve the purpose for which I sent it" (Isa 55:11).

What about Original Sin?

The Christian doctrine of original sin includes two basic notions. It is the sin that was first committed by Adam in the garden of Eden, and it also refers to sinful human nature that has been passed down from Adam to every person in every generation. Interestingly, the term original sin is not in the Bible. This theological doctrine was formulated by St. Augustine (354–430 AD), at a time when *de novo* creation of humanity was the science-of-the-day. Throughout history, the church has firmly upheld his understanding of original sin, and so too this ancient science of human origins. However, now that modern science offers a more accurate understanding of our origins, a re-evaluation of Augustine's doctrine is in order.

This situation is similar to the reinterpretation of biblical passages refer-ring to an immovable earth in the 1600s. When astronomers recognized that the earth rotated on its axis daily, theologians eventually appreciated a vital interpretive principle: The Book of Nature assists us in understand-ing the Book of Scripture.

In light of the scientific discovery of human evolution and recogni-tion of the ancient science in the biblical accounts of origins, it is clear that the *de novo* creation of Adam never happened, and as a consequence, all of humanity could not have descended from him. This is a very challenging notion for most Christians. However, this assertion is based on evidence from both the Book of God's Words and the Book of God's Works. Since Adam never existed, he could not have committed a first and original sin, and therefore, sin could not have been passed down from him to the rest of humanity. The implications for the traditional doctrine of original sin are significant, but ultimately not relevant to Christian faith or to our daily walk with the Lord.

Evolutionary creation proposes a reformulation of the notion of original sin. By applying the Message-Incident Principle (Fig 3-1, page 45), this position separates the Message of Faith in Gen 2 and 3—all hu-mans are sinners—from the underlying incidental ancient science of the *de novo* creation of Adam. Evolutionary creation then places this inerrant spiritual truth regarding human sinfulness within an incidental modern scientific vessel—the gradual evolution of humankind. Viewed in this way, the entrance of sin into the world did not come through one punctiliar event (i.e., at one point) committed by one individual. Instead, "original" sin was manifested gradually and mysteriously over many generations during the evolutionary processes leading to men and women. Thus, sin did originally enter the world, but not through Adam.

It must be underlined that theological formulations, like the tradi-tional doctrine of original sin and my own approach to this issue, have a human element, and therefore should always be open to revision as knowledge of Scripture and science advances. In addition, we must never lose sight of what's important. For example, I don't believe in the tradi-tional doctrine of original sin because I recognize that an ancient scien-tific element (the *de novo* creation of Adam) has been conflated with the Message of Faith (human sinfulness). But do I believe in sin, and am I a sinner? Absolutely. And do I believe that Jesus died for my sins? Again, absolutely, because "there is no other name under heaven [note the ancient astronomy] given to men by which we must be saved" (Acts 4:12). Once more, consider our development in the womb. I don't know when I first became a sinner. Did it happen at the moment my father's sperm cell fertilized my mother's egg cell? Or as an embryo with a yet to be developed brain? Or when I was an infant who did not understand right from wrong? I don't know. However, am I a sinner? Yes. Does it really matter knowing exactly when I became a sinner? No, I don't think so.

Human sinfulness is a non-negotiable principle of the Christian faith. As Scripture states, "All have sinned and fall short of the glory of God" (Rom 3:23). Knowing the details of *how* sin entered the world does not change the fact *that* we are sinners. But more importantly, let us always remember that Jesus entered the world and that He died for our sins, offering us the hope of eternal life. Amen!

What about Suffering and Death in Evolution?

A serious challenge faced by evolutionary creation is to justify why the all-loving and all-powerful God of the Bible would have created life, including humans, through a violent, wasteful, and senselessly competitive process like evolution. Extinction, natural selection, and survival of the fittest mark this creative method. For example, there have been five mass extinctions on earth. The last was 65 million years ago, when an asteroid the size of Manhattan hit our planet around the Yucatan Peninsula in Mexico. Two-thirds of all plants and animals were wiped out, as well as all the dinosaurs. Where was the Creator when this happened? Did the God of Love not have the power to deflect this asteroid away from the earth and save His creatures?

For many non-Christians, the presence today of meaningless suffering and death in the world is the main stumbling block to faith, and this aspect of biological evolution leads them further away from the Creator. Equally troubled, a number of Christians reject evolution on moral grounds. They argue that a Holy God would never use such a wicked and merciless process to create a "very good" world for humans made in the "Image of God" (Gen 1:27, 31). But the issue of suffering doesn't stop there for Christians. What are they to make of the morality of the excessively heavy-handed penalty for the sin of only one man? Has the entire creation been "groaning," "subjected to frustration," and in "bondage to decay" (Rom 8:20–22) because of one rebellious act in the garden of Eden? Do women experience excruciating pain during childbirth today because of one sin by Eve (Gen 3:16)? Is our inevitable death due to Adam at one time biting into the fruit of a forbidden tree? Does this reflect the justice of a Holy God?

The problem of suffering and death is quite a challenge for Christians, especially evolutionary creationists. Yet it must be underlined that the church has wrestled with this issue for nearly two thousand years, well before the discovery of biological evolution in the 1800s. In doing so, Christians have proposed numerous arguments, termed a "theodicy" (Greek *theos*: God, *dikē*: justice), that attempt to justify the presence of pain and mortality in a world created by an all-loving and all-powerful God. And history reveals that there are no easy quick-fix solutions.

This is an issue that I doubt anyone ever entirely comes to terms with. At best, theodicy is an intellectual tension for me. Let me explain this idea. Have you ever had a horrendous experience, one so bad that you'd never wish it upon your enemies? And now years later, when you look back at this event, can you say that there was something "good" about it, and that you're even "glad" you went through it? If you answer yes to both of these questions, like most people do, then your theodicy features two contrasting components held in an intellectual tension. This is essentially how I have come to terms with the God of Love creating a very good world through a ruthless evolutionary process.

Scripture and science also assist in putting the cruel mechanisms of evolution in perspective. Let me offer six examples that soften the bite of evolutionary mechanisms:

First, the ultimate purpose of the Christian faith must be considered in this discussion. Does the gospel message not include notions that could be termed "spiritual selection," "the survival of the spiritually fittest," and even "spiritual extinction?" On Judgment Day, are sheep not going to be separated from goats (Matt 25:31–46)? Will wheat not be brought into the barn whilst weeds are bundled and burned (Matt 13:24–30)? And those whose name is not in the Book of Life, are they not going to be thrown into the lake of fire (Rev 20:15)? Today, very few Christians relish the thought of eternal damnation. But it is a harsh reality ordained by the God of Love to serve His purpose in creating a body of individuals to enjoy eternity with Him. As believers come to terms with the reality that many will be lost forever, their justification for this gut-wrenching future reality can be applied to the evolutionary process, putting some divine perspective on extinction, natural selection, and the survival of the fittest.

Second, although evolution raises moral issues, Christians must never forget that the Bible reveals suffering and death as part of God's creative method in making a holy people. The creation of a territory for Israel to inhabit involved obeying the divine command to wipe out the people in the land of Canaan: "You must destroy them totally. Make no treaty with them and show them no mercy" (Deut 7:2). The violent and vicious character of Israel's invasion is typified by the fall of Jericho. Scripture records, "They devoted the city to the Lord and destroyed with the sword every living thing in it—men and women, young and old, cattle, sheep and donkeys" (Josh 7:21). And the Bible acknowledges God's part in the ruthless destruction of this city. In setting up the attack, the Lord said to Joshua, "See, I have delivered Jericho into your hands" (Josh 6:2). Most would agree that the agony and terror launched upon this city was not only excessive, but even senseless. Why waste animals and murder innocent children? As you attempt to answer this question, you will see that the moral issues surrounding evolution simply pale away.

Third, God's creative method in making each of us offers further insight into evolutionary pain and mortality. Science reveals that the processes of reproduction and development include wastage, competition, suffering, and death. Every menstrual cycle destroys an egg, blood, and womb tissue. Millions of sperm cells are wasted in every ejaculation, and after a competitive race to the egg, only one is necessary for fertilization. Most notably, 50% of fertilized eggs die in the womb. (Another unanswerable question arises: What is their eternal status?) Pregnancy is often difficult and birth, excruciatingly painful. And the death of cells is even programmed into genes. Termed "apoptosis," it is an indispensable creative mechanism during embryological development. For example, if the tissue between finger bones did not die, our hands would only be paddles. In other words, cell death is an ordained and sustained natural process used by God in "knitting us together in our mother's womb" to become "fearfully and wonderfully made" (Ps 139:13–14). In light of these reproductive and developmental facts, it is possible to view pain, wastage, and death as essential components in the Lord's evolutionary method.

Fourth, Scripture and environmental science also assist in providing perspective on suffering and death in the biological world. Ecologists have shown that predation is absolutely necessary in sustaining life on earth, and the Bible claims that it is part of God's good plan. In fact, the psalmist sees the Creator's providential activity in feeding all creatures, including those that prey on others.

> You [God] bring darkness, it becomes night,
>   and all the beasts of the forest prowl.
> The lions roar for their prey
>   and seek their food from God. . . .
> There is the sea, vast and spacious,
>   teeming with creatures beyond number—
>   living things both large and small. . . .
> These all look to You to give them
>   their food at the proper time.
> When You give it to them, they gather it up;
>   when You open Your hand,
>   they are satisfied with good things.
>
>   Psalm 104: 20–21, 25, 27–28

> The eyes of all look to You [God],
>   and You give them their food at the proper time.
> You open Your hand and satisfy the desires
>   of every living thing.
> The Lord is righteous in all His ways and loving
>   to all He has made.
>
>   Psalm 145:15–17

Many will find it difficult to believe that predatory attacks are "loving," "righteous," and "good things." However, the biblical writers knew of the violent nature of lions. These animals "strangle" (Nah 2:12) and "devour prey" (Num 23:24), "break bones" (Isa 38:13), "maul and mangle" (Mic 5:8), and "rip and tear to pieces" (Ps 7:2). Even so, Scripture indicates that predation is part of God's ordained and sustained plan. Thus, Christians need to re-evaluate their assumptions about the notion of "goodness" as it relates to the biological world. In this way, the suffering and death associated with evolution can be viewed in a new light, and can even be seen as a good aspect of the Lord's method of creation.

Fifth, Jesus offers a divine perspective on the issue of theodicy that can be applied to evolution. He advances the radical notion that there is purpose in suffering and death. The gospel of John records:

As Jesus went along, He saw a man blind from birth. His disciples asked him, "Rabbi, who sinned, this man or his parents, that he was born blind?" "Neither this man nor his parents sinned," said Jesus, "but this happened so that the work of God might be displayed in his life."

John 9:1–3

Shockingly, the Lord reveals that the man's suffering was meant to glorify God. This is not a heartless disregard for the pain caused by a birth defect, because Jesus certainly identified with human agony. For example, after Lazarus' death, He was "deeply moved in spirit and troubled," and He "wept" (John 11:33, 35). Yet earlier Jesus had proclaimed that Lazarus' "sickness will not end in death. No, it is for God's glory so that God's Son may be glorified through it" (11:4). Indeed, the raising of Lazarus, like the healing of the man born blind, glorified God because it showed His sovereign reign over suffering and death. And notably, in both of these cases, Jesus had the perfect opportunity to claim that Adam's sin in Gen 3 was at the root of pain and mortality. But He never did. Thus, in the light of Christ, we have biblical precedent to view the harsh mechanisms of evolution as purposeful and God-glorifying aspects of His creative method.

Finally, the apostle Paul offers insight into suffering and death from a future and eternal point of view. Despite his observation that the entire creation has been "groaning," "subjected to frustration," and in "bondage to decay" (Rom 8:20–22), he argues that "our present sufferings are not worth comparing with the glory that will be revealed in us" (v. 19). In fact, a few verses later, Paul concludes that "all things work together for good for those who love God" (v. 28). As challenging as it might be for many Christians to accept, "all things" include suffering and death, and consequently, these harsh realities actually "work together for good." Of course, it takes much perspective to grasp this notion. And since evolution is a fact of nature, "all things" extend to evolutionary suffering and death. Such a radical idea can only be understood from an eternal and divine perspective. Let me explain.

As noted earlier in this chapter, I believe that the Creator has made an ideal world with the primary intention of having men and women come into a personal and loving relationship with Him. This is a creation in which God does not crush us with His presence, or force us to believe in Him. He has given us genuine freedom in order to express genuine love. It is also a world in which the Lord demands faith. To be sure, nature features many ruthless characteristics, but these are essential factors that contribute to creating an environment where humans have a real choice to believe or disbelieve in God. An evolutionary process free of suffering and death would be similar to the fossil pattern predictions of young earth creation and progressive creation. There would be no debate. Evolution would be like a computer program with no glitches, proving without any doubt the existence of a Programmer. Such a world would undermine human freedom and disrupt faith, destroying the Creator's ultimate purpose—the creation of human beings to enjoy His love.

In an evolutionary creation, people are free to focus their attention on the brutal aspects of evolution, like countless extinctions, natural selection, and survival of the fittest. And some have, leading them to deism, agnosticism, and atheism. However, I contend that the amazing reflections of intelligent design in "all things," including the mechanisms of evolution, *overwhelmingly override* the merciless character of evolution, and point to the existence of God. Yet as the Metaphysics-Physics Principle indicates, I recognize that believing the Creator is behind the evolutionary process still requires a step of faith. Or to rephrase Scripture in modern terms: it is by faith I understand that the universe evolved at God's command (Heb 11:3).

What Do We Teach in Our Churches and Schools?

Among the most important and challenging aspects of the origins debate are the practical issues that arise. Recognizing the emphasis that many Christians place on this topic, how are we to deal with the diversity of views found in our churches? What position on origins are we to preach from our pulpits and teach in our Sunday schools and Christian educational institutions? Outside the church, is it the duty of believers to force publicly funded school boards and privately owned publishing houses to include their view of origins in curricula and textbooks? And when witnessing to non-Christians, should we impose our understanding of God's creative method and include it as an essential part of the Gospel? Of course, these questions could become the subject of a number of books. I certainly do not have all the answers. But here are a few preliminary thoughts.

The origins debate is often a divisive issue in our churches. To keep harmony within a fellowship, some pastors refuse to discuss the topic. Such an approach avoids unnecessary confrontations, but history reveals that believers have always raised questions about the creation of the world. It is a subject too important to ignore. The apostle Paul offers wisdom that is applicable to this situation. A significant theme in his letters warns against divisions in the body of Christ (Rom 16:17; 1 Cor 1:10,

11:18, 12:25; Titus 3:10). Using this admonition today, we should never be divided because of our views on how God created the universe and life. Let this issue be a difference among us. Proverbs 27:17 states, "As iron sharpens iron, so one man sharpens another." Instead of dividing us, the origins debate offers an opportunity to learn from one another and to develop a better understanding of the revelations in God's Two Books. And most importantly, we must never lose perspective. No origins position should ever be conflated with the Cross of Christ. Nothing other than our sin should be nailed to the Cross.

Another important pastoral theme found in the letters of Paul deals with the problem of stumbling blocks. In particular, he calls on mature Christians not to let the eating of food sacrificed to idols become an issue, since this practice was an obstacle for some believers (Rom 14:1–3, 13–17; 1 Cor 11:31–33). Similarly, I do not think that origins should be a central topic in any church. Focusing on God's creative method in Sunday morning sermons distracts people from the inerrant messages in Scripture and invites unnecessary controversy. However, I do believe that Sunday schools and Christian schools must introduce students to the various positions of origins, including evolutionary creation. If at some point young men and women ever accept evolution, then they will have a category that protects them from stumbling and losing their faith. As I mentioned earlier, I have personally lived through that disastrous spiritual situation because of a class on evolution during my freshman year of college; and I have seen it happen too often to students at the university where I teach.

Christians with a solid grasp of the spectrum of origins positions are also equipped to dismiss the popular myth, held by many non-Christians, that coming to Christ requires the rejection of evolution. Regrettably, too many anti-evolutionists have set this stumbling block between the Lord and those in dire need of Him. Let us for a moment assume that God created life through an evolutionary process, and that non-Christian scientists see the physical evidence supporting biological evolution every day in their laboratories. Is there any doubt that a terrible obstacle to faith has been set in front of them by young earth creationists and progressive creationists? As the apostle Paul writes, "Now is the time of God's favor, now is the day of salvation. We put no stumbling block in anyone's path, so that our ministry will not be discredited" (2 Cor 6:2–3). Anti-evolutionism should never be placed between any person and Jesus.

The next few comments are rather incisive. I have concerns with regard to public education in the nation. For example, consider the 1995 "Statement on Teaching Evolution" prepared by the National Association of Biology Teachers. The first point in this declaration states:

> The diversity of life on earth is the outcome of evolution: an unsupervised, impersonal, unpredictable and natural process of temporal descent with genetic modification that is affected by natural selection, chance, historical contingencies and changing environments.[2]

This statement conflates evolutionary science with a dysteleological worldview, and in the eyes of unsuspecting teachers and students, it "baptizes" this atheistic belief with scientific authority. Anti-evolutionists have been absolutely correct in objecting to the misuse of public funds for such an insidious indoctrination of children with this distinctly godless and anti-Christian ideology. In a democratic society, public education must reflect the views and intentions of the American people, and not the dysteleological and humanist beliefs of a skewed dictatorial minority.

In fact, the founding document of the United States, the *Declaration of Independence*, not only affirms the existence of a Creator, but accepts that He acts providentialistically in the world, and that He is the basis for morality and human rights.[3] Moreover, about 95% of Americans are united in affirming that there is a God or Universal Spirit.[4] Thus, any government-funded institution that aggressively undermines belief in the Creator outlined in the *Declaration* betrays the nation. The promotion in public education of dysteleological evolution and secular humanism is an attack on the metaphysical foundations of America. Stated precisely and without any regard to political correctness, those indoctrinating children with a purposeless worldview are enemies of the union.

Once again, the apostle Paul offers valuable insight and advice that is applicable to this situation today. He affirms the reality of ongoing spiritual warfare:

> For though we live in this world, we do not wage war as the world does. The weapons we fight with are not the weapons of the world. On the contrary, they have divine power to demolish strongholds. We demolish arguments and every pretension that sets itself up against the knowledge of God.
>
> 2 Corinthians 10:3–5

A modern day stronghold set up against the knowledge of God is any publicly funded school system dedicated to brainwashing children with atheistic evolution and godless humanism. American Christians have every democratic right to eradicate this spiritual darkness from public education.

I opened this subsection acknowledging that I definitely do not have all the answers to the many pastoral and educational issues that arise from the origins debate. This is an opportunity for a lot of creative thinking on the part of ministers and teachers. After having taught this controversy for over ten years at a publicly funded university, I have come to the conclusion that good education exposes students to all positions and categories. I believe that this is a good pastoral principle as well. My teaching experience has also shown me that the origins debate provides an excellent forum for developing critical thinking skills and an integrated worldview. In this way, young men and women are liberated from the prison of the origins dichotomy into which most have been socially conditioned. And now they are free to enjoy both the God-glorifying evidence in science and the life-changing truths in Scripture.

What about Dinosaurs, How Do They Fit into the Bible?

The time has come to return to the story presented in the preface of this book and to answer directly the question a high school student asked one of America's leading anti-evolutionists: "What about dinosaurs, how do they fit into the Bible?" The answer is simple: they don't. Scripture features an ancient science, and dinosaurs are part of modern science. This question is like asking, how do NASA rockets fit into the Bible? Or where do telescopes and microscopes come in? Or how does evolution fit into Scripture? None do. I am sure that most readers will now appreciate why I did not give this answer to that student. He would not have understood, and it would only have confused him further. So, I accommodated and I affirmed his godly faith and courage to ask such an excellent question. I believe this was the right thing to do at that volatile moment.

Of course, the assumption behind this high school student's question is scientific concordism. He took it for granted that dinosaurs *had* to fit into the Bible.[5] But as the epigraph of this book reveals, one of the most beloved preachers in America recognizes that this common interpretive approach is an error. Billy Graham confesses that Christians "have misinterpreted the Scriptures many times and we've tried to make the

Scriptures say things that they weren't meant to say . . . we have made a mistake by thinking the Bible is a scientific book. The Bible is not a book of science."[6] Or to restate Graham's observation, scientific concordism is a mistake. And who hasn't made a mistake interpreting Scripture? I have made more than my fair share. Proof that Christians have often misinterpreted Scripture is the fact that most of our churches and Christian schools still teach young earth creation and progressive creation. But as I have argued in previous chapters, these anti-evolutionary views of origins do not align with the evidence in the Book of God's Works (Figs 4-3, 4-5, 4-8; pages, 84, 88, 91, respectively).

Instead of being a divine revelation of scientific facts, Reverend Graham correctly underlines that "the Bible is a book of Redemption." It convicts us of our sinfulness and offers the hope of eternal life through the sacrificial death of Jesus on the Cross. Using professional definitions of the terms creation and evolution, Graham states, "I accept the Creation story. I believe that God created man, and whether it came by an evolutionary process and at a certain point He took this person or being and made him a living soul or not, does not change the fact that God did create man."[7] In other words, creation refers simply to that which the Creator has made, and evolution only to a natural process—period. Graham does not make the error of conflating creation with young earth creation or evolution with atheism. With perfect perspective, he then concludes that "whichever way God did it [created] makes no difference as to what man is and man's relationship to God."[8] And for well over half a century, Billy Graham has preached brilliantly from the Book of God's Words the Messages of Faith that we are the only creatures created in the Image of God, we have all fallen into sin, and Jesus has died for our sins so that we can enjoy a personal relationship with Him.

I have the greatest respect for Doctor Graham's intellectual integrity. He is not a scientist, and he doesn't pretend to be, unlike some leading anti-evolutionists we see today who are lawyers, philosophers, historians, etc. Consequently, Graham is open to the possibility of biological evolution, including the evolution of humans, should the scientific facts lead him in that direction. Why? Because "it makes no difference." Clearly, he has peace regarding origins. I think that it is important for Christians who are not familiar with the scientific evidence for evolution to embrace Graham's attitude and to be at peace with this issue. It's okay not to know how God made the universe and life. Personally, as a Christian I have held a wide variety of positions—young earth creation, a hazy form of progressive creation, and evolutionary creation. Yet despite my struggles to understand this issue, Jesus has always been at my side as Lord and Savior. Like Billy Graham, I have learned over time that the purpose of Scripture is to reveal *that* God created, and not *how* He created.

So let's conclude and put origins in perspective. How important is this issue? At one level it is absolutely irrelevant. Knowing how God created the world is not essential to being or becoming a Christian. Most believers throughout history had no idea that the earth was billions of years old or that living creatures had evolved. Yet they were able to enjoy a personal relationship with the Lord Jesus. At another level, the issue of origins is absolutely relevant because people today want to know how the world came into existence. We live in a scientific society and Bible-believing Christians will inevitably inquire about the relationship between Scripture and science. In particular, there is a younger generation that is asking, "What about dinosaurs, how do they fit into the Bible?" We must attempt to offer an answer, because we don't want any of them to stumble and lose their faith over this issue, as I did in my first year of college. Hopefully, I've given a few reasonable suggestions in this book. And yes, I have come to one very surprising conclusion. I love Jesus and I accept evolution. But more importantly, as the children's Sunday school song has taught me, "Jesus loves me, this I know, for the Bible tells me so."

Notes

Preface

1. Billy Graham, "Doubts and Certainties: David Frost interview" BBC-2, 1964, in David Frost, *Billy Graham: Personal Thoughts of a Public Man. 30 years of Conversations with David Frost* (Colorado Springs: Chariot Victor, 1997), 73–74.

Chapter One

1. Edward J. Larson and Larry Witham, "Scientists Are Still Keeping the Faith" *Nature* 386 (3 Apr 1997), 435–36.

2. Charles R. Darwin, *On the Origin of Species. A Facsimile of the First Edition.* Introduced by Ernst Mayr. (Cambridge: Harvard University Press, 1964 [1859]), 488. For other appearances of the term Creator, see 186, 188, 189, 413 (twice), 435.

3. Charles R. Darwin, *The Life and Letters of Charles Darwin.* Edited by Francis Darwin, 3 vols. (London: John Murray, 1887), 1:304.

4. A 2004 survey reveals that 87% of evangelical Protestants believe that Gen 1 is a literal word-for-word account of how God actually created the world. No Author, "Six in Ten Take Bible Stories Literally, But Don't Blame Jews for Death of Jesus." No pages. Survey conducted 6–10 February 2004 with a random sample of 1011 adults by ICR-International Communications Research Media, PA. Accessed July 6, 2006. Online: http://www.icrsurvey.com/studies/947a1%20Views%20of%20the%20Bible.pdf.

Chapter Two

1. See chapter 1 endnote 4.

2. Classic books include: Henry Morris and John Whitcomb, *The Genesis Flood: The Biblical Record and Its Scientific Implications* (Presbyterian & Reformed Press, 1961); Duane T. Gish, *Evolution: The Fossils Say No!* (San Diego: Creation-Life Publishers, 1972); Ken Ham, *The Lie: Evolution* (Green Forest, AR: Master Books, 1987).

3. Martin Luther, *Luther's Works. Lectures on Genesis: Chapters 1–5.* Jaroslav Pelikan, ed. (Saint Louis: Concordia Publishing House, 1958), 3, 5.

4. To cite a few, Rom 5:12–14; 1 Cor 15:21–22, 45–47; 2 Cor 11:3; 1 Tim 2:13–15; 2 Pet 2:4–5.

5. Henry M. Morris, "Strong Delusion," *Back to Genesis* (No. 133), in *Acts and Facts*

(January 2000) Institute for Creation Research, El Cajon, CA; *The Troubled Waters of Evolution* (San Diego: Creation Life Publishers, 1982), 75; Gish, *Evolution*, 10.

6. The leading progressive creationist today is Hugh Ross. See his *Creation and Time: A Biblical and Scientific Perspective on the Creation-Date Controversy* (Colorado Springs: NavPress, 1994) and *The Genesis Question: Scientific Advances and the Accuracy of Genesis* (Colorado Springs: NavPress, 1998).

7. This origins position is only beginning to be defined. See Keith B. Miller, ed., *Perspectives on an Evolving Creation* (Grand Rapids: Eerdmans, 2003); Darrel R. Falk, *Coming to Peace with Science: Bridging the Worlds Between Faith and Biology* (Downer's Grove: InterVarsity Press, 2004); Francis S. Collins, *The Language of God: A Scientist Presents Evidence for Belief* (New York: Free Press, 2006).

8. My use of the term complementary is intentional. The Latin *complēre*, from which this word is derived, means "to finish" and "to fulfill." The verb "to complement" refers to the act of adding something that is lacking in order to make complete. From an evolutionary creationist perspective, Scripture and science finish or fulfill each other, making our understanding of origins complete.

9. See endnote 3 in chapter 1.

10. Today's leading dysteleological evolutionist is Richard Dawkins. See his *The Blind Watchmaker* (London: Penguin, 1986) and *The God Delusion* (New York: Houghton Mifflin, 2006).

11. No Author, "Religion Index Hits Ten-Year High," *Emerging Trends: Journal of the Princeton Religion Research Center* 18 (Mar 1996), 4.

CHAPTER THREE

1. This passage is from the NRSV. The NIV translates this verse as the mustard seed "is the smallest seed that *you plant* in the ground." However, the pronoun "you" and the verb "plant" are not in the original Greek or any variants. A similar attempt by the NIV to mitigate this scientific problem occurs with "the smallest of all *your seeds*" in Matt 13:32. Even the NIV interlinear does not support this rendition. See Alfred Marshall, *The New International Version Interlinear Greek-English New Testament* (Grand Rapids: Zondervan, 1976), 56; cf., 153.

2. The translations of Greek and Hebrew words in this book are common renditions from standard lexicons: Walter Bauer, *A Greek-English Lexicon of the New Testament and other Early Christian Literature*, William F. Arndt and F. Wilbur Gingrich, eds. (Chicago: University of Chicago Press, 1958); Henry George Liddell, *A Greek-English Lexicon*, revised by Henry Stuart Jones (Oxford: Oxford University Press, 1996); Francis Brown, S.R. Driver, and C.A. Briggs, *Hebrew and English Lexicon of the Old Testament* (Oxford: Clarendon Press, 1951).

3. Modern Bibles using the word "expanse" include the influential New International Version and New American Standard. However, Today's NIV (2002) employs "vault."

4. For literature on the 3-tier universe, see Stanley L. Jaki, *Genesis 1 Through the Ages* (London: Thomas Moore Press, 1992), 275–79; Lloyd R. Bailey, "The Cosmology of the Ancient Semites," in his *Genesis, Creation and Creationism* (New York: Paulist Press, 1993), 172–85; John H. Walton, *Ancient Near Eastern Thought and the Old Testament: Introducing the Conceptual World of the Hebrew Bible* (Grand Rapids: Baker Academic, 2006), 165–78; Paul H. Seely, *Inerrant Wisdom: Science and Inerrancy in Biblical Perspective* (Portland: Evangelical Reformed, 1989).

5. See Henry M. Morris, *Many Infallible Proofs*, 232, 242; Hugh Ross, "Biblical Forecasts of Scientific Discoveries." No pages. Accessed November 13, 2006. Online: http://www .reasons.org/resources/apologetics/forecasts.shtml

6. Eugene H. Peterson, *The Message: The New Testament in Contemporary Language* (Colorado: NavPress, 1993), title page.

7. For a similar Incarnational approach to understanding the nature of Scripture, see Peter Enns, *Inspiration and Incarnation: Evangelicals and the Problem of the Old Testament* (Grand Rapids: Baker Academic, 2005). See also Kenton L. Sparks, *God's Word in Human Words: An Evangelical Appropriation of Critical Biblical Scholarship* (Grand Rapids: Baker Academic, 2005).

8. Of course, a spore is technically not a seed since most are haploid. But I believe the analogy makes my point.

9. I am indebted to Ladd's aphorism, "The Bible is the Word of God given in the words of men in history." George Eldon Ladd, *New Testament and Criticism* (Grand Rapids: Eerdmans, 1967), 12.

CHAPTER FOUR

1. This survey asked American adults whether a Bible story was "literally true, meaning it happened that way word-for-word" or "meant as a lesson, but not to be taken literally." The biblical accounts included: (1) "The creation story in which the world was created in six days," (2) "The story of Noah and the ark in which it rained for 40 days and nights; the entire world was flooded; and only Noah, his family, and the animals on their ark survived." Sixty-one percent take the former literally, and sixty percent the latter. Eighty-seven percent of evangelical Protestants believe both accounts are literal records of events. No Author, "Six in Ten Take Bible Stories Literally, But Don't Blame Jews for Death of Jesus." No pages. Surveyed conducted 6–10 February 2004 with a random sample of 1011 adults by ICR-International Communications Research Media, PA. Accessed July 6, 2006. Online: http://www.icrsurvey.com/studies/947a1%20Views%20of%20the%20Bible.pdf.

2. For scholarly works defending the historicity of Gen 12–50, see Kenneth A. Kitchen, *On the Reliability of the Old Testament* (Grand Rapids: Eerdmans, 2003); Ian W. Provan, Philips V. Long and Tremper Longman III, *A Biblical History of Israel* (Louisville: Westminster John Knox Press, 2003).

3. See pages 57–59 regarding the existence of the firmament and waters above after the flood. These structures did not collapse during the deluge, as suggested by young earth creationists.

4. See David Adams Leeming and Margaret Adams Leeming, *Encyclopedia of Creation Myths* (Santa Barbara: ABC-CLIO, Inc., 1994).

5. Modern origins science also features this type of thinking, known as retrojection (Latin *retro*: backward; *jacere*: to throw). For example, we use known natural processes seen today in the earth's crust in order to explain geological evolution.

6. Attempts to restrict the adjective "all" creates more problems that it solves. For example, in Gen 1 it would mean "all" those creatures except the ones created in Gen 2, and in the latter chapter "all" those made in the garden of Eden. Not only does this produce two creative periods for birds, animals, vegetation, etc., but it also results in an inconsistent use of this adjective. A less tortuous approach is to suggest that Gen 1 and 2 are two separate origins accounts.

7. The suggestion that Gen 2:8, 19 are parenthetical comments that refer to previous creative acts in Gen 1 (e.g., the NIV's "Now the Lord God had . . .") is not supported by the Hebrew Bible. Both of these verses begin with the consecutive *waw* (translated "and") to indicate that the creative events are in a sequential order. Examine the NIV interlinear Hebrew-English Bible and contrast Gen 2:8, 19 with the use of the disjunctive *waw* (translated "now, but") in Gen 1:2 ("Now the earth was . . .").

8. These two sources are conventionally categorized as the Priestly (Gen 1) and Jahwist (Gen 2). But it is important to underline that my acceptance of sources is not an endorsement of Julius Wellhausen's Documentary (JEPD) Hypothesis. In recent years, this theory regarding the origin of the first five books of the Bible has come under much scholarly criticism. However, this is not to say that there were no written accounts employed in the inspiration of Scripture. For a more complete explanation about sources, see my *Evolutionary Creation*, 85–86, 403–10.

9. Stephanie Daley, *Myths from Mesopotamia* (Oxford: University Press, 1989), 4, 16–17; Walter Beyerlin, ed. *Near Eastern Religious Texts Relating to the Old Testament* (Philadelphia: Westminster Press, 1978), 76.

10. The lost idyllic age is sometimes referred to as the lost golden age. Mircea Eliade, one of the greatest scholars of comparative religions, states, "In more or less complex forms, the paradisiac myth occurs here and there all over the world." *Myths, Dreams and Mysteries* (New York: Harper and Row, 1967), 59. He refers to the loss of the paradisiacal age as "the fall" and "the fall of man." Ibid., 60, 63, 66. See also "The Perfection of the Beginnings" in his *Myth and Reality* (New York: Harper and Row, 1963), 50–53; Richard Heinberg, *Memories and Visions of Paradise: Exploring the Universal Myth of a Lost Golden Age* (Los Angeles: Jeremy P. Tarcher, Inc., 1989), 81–111; David Adams Leeming and Margaret Adams Leeming, *Encyclopedia of Creation Myths* (Santa Barbara: ABC-CLIO, Inc., 1994), viii.

11. Genesis 2–4 was composed by the same author. Compare Gen 3–4 with the literary features listed for Gen 2 on page 79.

12. James B. Pritchard, ed. *Ancient Near Eastern Texts Relating to the Old Testament*, 3rd ed. (Princeton: Princeton University Press, 1969), 38.

13. For my approach to the biblical flood, see *Evolutionary Creation*, 183–84, 216–17, 277–81.

CHAPTER FIVE

1. Henry M. Morris, *The Troubled Waters of Evolution* (San Diego: Creation-Life Publishers, 1982), 75.

2. The scientific information in this section appears in standard geological textbooks. Accessible introductions on the age of the earth written by Christians include: Davis A. Young and Ralph F. Stearley, *The Bible, Rocks, and Time* (Downers Grove: IVP Academic, 2008); Hugh Ross, *Creation and Time* (Colorado Springs: NavPress, 1994); Hugh Ross, *A Matter of Days* (Colorado Springs: NavPress, 1994). I am grateful to geologists Martin Unsworth and Murray Gingras for their assistance.

3. A. Hornbruch and L. Wolpert, "Positional Signaling by Henson's Node when Grafted to the Chick Limb," *Journal of Experimental Morphology* 94 (1986), 257–65; Scott F. Gilbert, *Developmental Biology*, 8th ed. (Sunderland: Sinauer, 2006), 518–24.

4. A. S. Tucker, K. L. Matthews, and P. T. Sharpe, "Transformation of Tooth Type Induced by Inhibition of BMP Signaling," *Science* 282 (1998), 1136–38.

5. G. Halder, P. Callaerts, and W.J. Gehring, "Induction of Ectopic Eyes by Targeted Expression of the Eyeless Gene in Drosophila," *Science* 267 (1995), 1788–92.

6. Matthew P. Harris, Sean M. Hasso, Mark W.J. Ferguson, and John F. Fallon, "The Development of Archosaurian First-Generation Teeth in a Chicken Mutant," *Current Biology* 16 (2006), 371–77.

7. Yiping Chen, Yanding Zhang, and Ting-Xing Jiang, "Conservation of Early Odontogenic Signaling Pathways in *Aves*," *Proceedings of the National Academy of Science* 97 (2000), 10044–49.

8. E.J. Kollar and C. Fisher, "Tooth Induction in Chick Epithelium: Expression of Quiescent Genes for Enamel Synthesis," *Science* 207 (1980), 993–95.

9. See footnote 6.

10. For an introduction to whale evolution, see Carl Zimmer, *At the Water's Edge: Macroevolution and the Transformation of Life* (New York: Free Press, 1998).

CHAPTER SIX

1. For the citation, see endnote 1 in chapter 4. Gallup Polls (1982, 1993, 1997, 1999, 2001, 2004, 2006) also reveal that between 44–47% of American adults believe that "God created human beings pretty much in their present form at one time within the last 10,000 years or so." No Author, "Science and Nature." No pages. Accessed December 23, 2006. Online: http://www.pollingreport.com/science.htm.

2. Two excellent introductions with striking pictures of pre-human fossils include: Paul F. Whitehead, William K. Sacco, and Susan B. Hochgraf, *A Photographic Atlas for Physical Anthropology* (Englewood, CO: Morton Publishing Company, 2005); Donald Johanson and Blake Edgar, *From Lucy to Language* (New York: Simon and Schuster, 2006).

3. Accessible introductions to genetics and evolution by Christians include: Francis S. Collins, *The Language of God: A Scientist Presents Evidence for Belief* (New York: Free Press, 2006), 124–42; Darrel R. Falk, *Coming to Peace with Science: Bridging the Worlds between Faith and Science* (Downers Grove: InterVarsity Press, 2004), 169–98; Graeme Finlay, *God's Books: Genetics & Genesis* (Auckland: TELOS Publications, 2004).

4. Based on Patricia C. Rice, *Biological Anthropology and Prehistory: Exploring Our Human Ancestry* (Boston: Pearson Education, 2005); Kenneth L. Feder, *The Past in Perspective: An Introduction to Human Prehistory*, 3rd ed. (New York: McGraw-Hill, 2004); William A. Haviland, *Human Evolution and Prehistory*, 6th ed. (Toronto: Wadsworth/ Thompson Learning, 2003). I am grateful to anthropologists Pamela Willoughby and Anne Holden for their assistance.

5. Some use Ps 51:5 to argue that humans are sinners from conception: "Surely I have been a sinner from birth, sinful from the time my mother conceived me." However, it is methodologically precarious to build a doctrine on only one verse. Moreover, this Psalm is highly figurative. David asks God to wash him "whiter than snow" and to "let the bones You have crushed rejoice" (v. 7–8). Therefore, he is employing hyperbole in order to underline his sinfulness in verse 5, not to offer a theological statement on the origin of sin in humans.

6. This category must be contrasted with *Traditional Monogenism*, which is the literal *de novo* creation of Adam from the dust of the ground and the creation of Eve using flesh from his side as described in Gen 2:7, 22.

7. For an explanation of the extremely long lifespans in Gen 5, see my book *Evolutionary Creation*, 211–14, 235–38.

8. See my comments on this point in the next chapter on pages 154–56.

CHAPTER SEVEN

1. For an excellent defense of this notion, see Richard Bauckham, *Jesus and the Eyewitnesses: The Gospels as Eyewitness Testimony* (Grand Rapids: Eerdmans, 2006).

2. National Association of Biology Teachers, "Statement on Teaching Biology," *American Biology Teacher* 58 (1995), 61. In fairness to the NABT, the statement was modified in 1997 (though not completely purged of dysteleological nuances) by removing the words "impersonal" and "unsupervised." Nevertheless my point remains: it is shocking that such a philosophically naive and skewed statement was ever published by such an important educational organization.

3. The *Declaration* makes four references to the Creator: "Nature's God," "their [humanity's] Creator," "the Supreme Judge of the world," and "divine Providence."

4. For citation, see endnote 11 in chapter 2.

5. Some readers might wonder whether this student was asking about the purported references to dinosaurs in Job 40–41. He never mentioned these passages. Like the circle of the earth (Is 40:22) and the suspension of the earth over nothing (Job 26:7; see excursus, pages 63–64), the so-called "dinosaur" interpretations are eisegetical and read modern scientific notions into the Bible. Dinosaurs went extinct 65 million years ago, and there is no evidence whatsoever of them existing in Job's day. If the latter were the case, we would find their bones in geological strata after the K-T Boundary and right up until today. But none exist after the asteroid impact 65 million years ago. Moreover, the descriptions of the creatures in these passages likely refer to an elephant or hippopotamus in Job 40:15–24, and to a crocodile in Job 41:1–34. See *New International Version Study Bible* (Grand Rapids: Zondervan, 2002), 774–75. I am grateful to Anthony Maiolo for his assistance.

6. Billy Graham, "Doubts and Certainties: David Frost interview" BBC-2, 1964, in David Frost, *Billy Graham: Personal Thoughts of a Public Man. 30 years of Conversations with David Frost* (Colorado Springs: Chariot Victor, 1997), 73.

7. Ibid.

8. Ibid., 74.

Credits

Fig 3-5. Babylonian World Map. Redrawn by Kenneth Kully, from Jeremy Black and Anthony Green, *Gods, Demons and Symbols of Ancient Mesopotamia: An Illustrated Dictionary* (Austin: University of Texas, 1992), 53; Lloyd R. Bailey, *Genesis, Creation and Creationism* (New York: Paulist Press, 1993), 174.

Fig 4-6. Shark Jaw and Teeth. Lower jaw of shark. Charles S. Tomes, *A Manual of Dental Anatomy* (London: A. & J. Churchill, 1898), 240. Single shark teeth redrawn by Braden Barr, from Robert L. Carroll, *Vertebrate Paleontology and Evolution* (New York: W.H. Freeman and Company, 1988), 68.

Fig 4-7. *Tyrannosaurus Rex* Skull and Teeth. T-Rex skull courtesy of Tracy Ford.

Fig 5-2. Radiometric Dating and Geological Stratification. Drawn by Braden Barr.

Fig 5-4. Reconstruction of Pangaea. Redrawn from Edward J. Tarbuck, Fredrick K. Lutgens, and Cameron J. Tsujita, *Earth: An Introduction to Physical Geology*, Canadian Edition (Toronto: Pearson Education, 2005), 515.

Fig 5-5. Sea Floor Expansion. Redrawn from Harold L. Levin, *Contemporary Physical Geology* (Philadelphia: Saunders, 1986), 271.

Fig 5-6. The Mid-Atlantic Ridge. Redrawn from Harold L. Levin, *Contemporary Physical Geology* (Philadelphia: Saunders, 1986), 281.

Fig 5-7. Lobe-Finned Fish and Early Amphibian. Redrawn by Andrea Dmytrash, from Robert L. Carroll, *Patterns and Processes of Vertebrate Evolution* (Cambridge: University Press, 1998), 300.

Fig 5-8. Labyrinthodont Tooth. Drawn by Braden Barr.

Fig 5-9. Fin to Limb Evolution. Redrawn by Andrea Dmytrash. Lobe-finned fish from M. I. Coates, J. E. Jeffrey and M. Rut, "Fins to Limbs: What the Fossils Say," *Evolution and Development* 4 (2002), 392; fish with fingers from Edward B. Daeschler and Neil Shubin, "Fish with Fingers?" *Nature* 391 (8 Jan 1997), 133; early amphibian from Robert L. Carroll, *Patterns and Processes of Vertebrate Evolution* (Cambridge: University Press, 1998), 233.

Fig 5-10. Experimental Limbs. Drawn by Kenneth Kully, from A. Hornbruch and L. Wolpert, "Positional Signaling by Henson's Node when Grafted to the Chick Limb," *Journal of Experimental Morphology* 94 (1986), 261.

Fig 5-11. Reptile to Mammal Dental Evolution. Redrawn by Braden Barr, from Robert L. Carroll, *Vertebrate Paleontology and Evolution* (New York: W.H. Freeman and Company, 1988), 196, 365, 386, 406, 408.

Fig 5-12. Reptile to Mammal Jaw Evolution. Redrawn by Andrea Dmytrash. Top three jaws from Robert L. Carroll, *Vertebrate Paleontology and Evolution* (New York: W.H. Freeman and Company, 1988), 366, 382, 390; bottom jaw from Kenneth D. Rose, *The Beginning of the Age of Mammals* (Baltimore: John Hopkins University Press, 2006), 92.

Fig 5-13. Tooth Development Stages. Drawn by Kenneth Kully.

Fig 5-14. Feathered Dinosaur. Reprinted with permission. Gregory S. Paul, *Dinosaurs of the Air: The Evolution and Loss of Flight in Dinosaurs and Birds* (Baltimore: Johns Hopkins University Press, 2002), 67.

Fig 5-15. The Teeth and Upper Jaw of the Famed Ancient Bird *Archaeopteryx*. Redrawn by Braden Barr, from M.E. Howgate, "The Teeth of Archaeopteryx and a reinterpretation of the Eichstätt specimen," *Zoological Journal of the Linnean Society* 82 (1984), 164.

Fig 5-16. Lower Leg Evolution and Development. Redrawn by Kenneth Kully, from Douglas J. Futuyma, *Evolutionary Biology*, 2nd ed. (Sunderland, MA: Sinauer Associates, 1986), 435.

Fig 5-17. Hen's Tooth Experiment. Drawn by Kenneth Kully.

Fig 5-18. Modern Toothed and Non-Tooth Whales. Killer whale teeth. Reprinted, no permission required (book published in 1898). Charles S. Tomes, *A Manual of Dental Anatomy* (London: A. & J. Churchill, 1898), 377. Bowhead whale. Reprinted, no permission required (book published in 1904). Max Weber, *Die Säugetiere* (Jena: Von Gustav Fischer, 1904), 555, 558.

Fig 5-19. Ancient Whales. Redrawn by Andrea Dmytrash, from Kenneth D. Rose, *The Beginning of the Age of Mammals* (Baltimore: Johns Hopkins University Press, 2006), 282.

Fig 5-20. Teeth and Upper Jaw of a Mesonychid and an Early Whale. Redrawn by Andrea Dmytrash, from Robert L. Carroll, *Patterns and Processes of Vertebrate Evolution* (Cambridge: University Press, 1998), 330, 335.

Fig 5-21. Foetal Teeth of Modern Non-Toothed Whales. Redrawn by Braden Barr, from A. E. W. Miles and Caroline Grigson, *Colyer's Variations and Diseases of the Teeth of Animals* (Cambridge: University Press, 1990), 101.

Fig 6-2. Similarities in Skeletons. Monkey skeleton. Daris R. Swindler, *Introduction to the Primates* (Seattle: University of Washington Press, 1998), 143. Reprinted with permission of University of Washington Press. Gorilla and human skeletons. Roger Lewin, *Human Evolution: An Illustrated Introduction*, 2nd ed. (Cambridge, MA: Blackwell Scientific Publications, 1989), 65. Reprinted with permission of Blackwell Scientific Publications.

Fig 6-3. Similarities in Rib Cages and Hip Bones. Chimpanzee, *A. afarensis* and human ribs and hips. William A. Haviland, Dana Walrath, Harald E. L. Prins and Bunny McBride, *Evolution and Prehistory: The Human Challenge*, (with info Trac®) 7th ed. (Toronto: Wadsworth/ Thompson Learning, 2005), 154; Fig 6.7. Reprinted with permission of Wadsworth, a division of Thompson Learning: www.thomsonrights.com. Fax 800–730–2215.

Fig 6-4. Similarities in Dentitions. Chimpanzee, *A. afarensis* and human dentitions. Roger Lewin, *Human Evolution: An Illustrated Introduction*, 2nd ed. (Cambridge, MA: Blackwell Scientific Publications, 1989), 70. Reprinted with permission of Blackwell Scientific Publications.

Fig 6-9. Evolution of Skulls in Pre-Humans and Humans. Artwork © copyright D. J. Maizels, 1994.

Glossary

Argument from Design. An argument for the existence of God that appeals to the beauty, complexity, and functionality seen in nature. See also **Intelligent Design**.

Atheism. The belief that God does not exist.

Concordism. A popular interpretive approach to the Bible that suggests there is a correspondence or alignment between Scripture and modern science. In this book, the term is expanded in order to distinguish accord between: (1) the Bible and the spiritual realm—theological concordism, and (2) the Bible and the physical world—scientific concordism. See also **Scientific Concordism**.

Conflation of Ideas. The collapsing of distinct ideas into one single notion. For example, the scientific theory of evolution is often conflated with the secular philosophy of atheism, leading many to assume that evolution can only be a godless and purposeless natural process.

Cosmic Fall. The belief that the physical world was dramatically changed after the entrance of human sin. God launched suffering, decay, and death upon the whole creation in judgment for the sin of Adam in the garden of Eden.

Creation. The basic belief that the universe and life is the product of a Creator. The doctrine of creation, as held by professional theologians, makes no reference as to the method through which God created.

Deism. The belief in an impersonal god. He created the world, but never enters it to interact with humans.

***De Novo* Creation**. God's dramatic creative action that results in fully formed inanimate things and living beings. For example, the creation of the universe and life in six 24-hour days. See also **Interventionism**.

Dichotomy of Ideas. The division of an issue into only two simple positions. An either/or approach to a topic. Some dichotomies are *true dichotomies*. For example, the world is either purposeful or purposeless. However, many dichotomies are *false dichotomies* because most issues are not limited to only two simple positions. The popular view of the origins debate is often confined to either creation in six 24-hour days or evolution by blind chance. This book argues that this assumption is a false dichotomy.

Dysteleology. The belief that the world has no ultimate plan or purpose. Existence is ultimately meaningless and driven only by blind chance.

Evolution. The scientific theory that the universe and life, including humans, arose through natural processes. Though this term usually refers to the evolution of life (biological evolution), it is also applied to the natural mechanisms producing galaxies, stars and planets (cosmological evolution), and the earth (geological evolution). The use of the term evolution by professional scientists makes no reference at all as to whether these natural processes are purposeful (teleological) or purposeless (dysteleological). Therefore, qualification of this term is often necessary. See also **Macro-Evolution**; **Micro-Evolution**; **Metaphysics**; **Dysteleology**; **Teleology**.

God-of-the-Gaps. God's dramatic action into the physical world in order to add missing parts in the original creation or correct natural processes that have gone astray. For example, God intervening to put planets back on their proper course. See also **Interventionism**.

Humanism (Secular Humanism). An ethical position that places humanity in the role traditionally held by God as the only determiner of values and morals.

Intelligent Design. The traditional belief that the beauty, complexity, and functionality in nature reflect the rational mind of a Creator. See also **Argument from Design**.

Interventionism. God's action in the world that is dramatic and breaks normal routine. See also **God-of-the-Gaps; Providentialism.**

Macro-Evolution. The scientific theory that all living organisms arose through evolutionary processes. For example, fish evolved into amphibians, amphibians into reptiles, reptiles into mammals, and mammals into humans. See also **Evolution; Micro-Evolution.**

Metaphysics. Beliefs regarding the ultimate meaning of the world. The Greek noun *phusis* refers to nature, and the preposition *meta* means behind, beyond, and after. Metaphysics deal with ultimate beliefs behind and beyond the physical world after it has been studied by science. Metaphysical ideas include non-physical concepts in philosophy and religion. For example, the Image of God and human sin are not scientific notions, but metaphysical beliefs. See also **Teleology; Dysteleology.**

Micro-Evolution. The anti-evolutionary theory that living organisms can only evolve to a limited extent. For example, a dog changing into another variety of dog, but it remains a dog. Micro-evolution rejects the macro-evolution of fish into amphibians, amphibians into reptiles, reptiles into mammals, and mammals into humans. See also **Evolution; Macro-Evolution.**

Providentialism. God's action in the world that is subtle and works through normal routine. See also **Interventionism.**

Scientific Concordism. Commonly known as concordism, this is a popular interpretive approach to the Bible that aligns modern science with statements in Scripture about the physical world. It assumes that the Holy Spirit revealed scientific facts to the biblical writers 1000s of years before their discovery by science. For example, the Day-Age Theory matches the creation days in Genesis 1 with geological periods in the history of the earth.

Teleology. The belief that the universe has an ultimate plan and purpose. For Christians, teleology is rooted in the God of the Bible.

Theism. The belief in a personal God who is in an intimate relationship with humans. Christians are theists who enjoy a personal relationship with the Lord Jesus.

Index

Lightning Source UK Ltd.
Milton Keynes UK
UKOW06f0019061016

284567UK00022BC/541/P